JAMES M. KOUZES

BARRY Z. POSNER

EDITORS

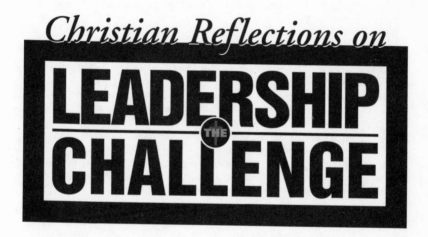

Christian Reflections on

LEADERSHIP THE CHALLENGE

FOREWORD BY
JOHN C. MAXWELL

JOSSEY-BASS
A Wiley Imprint
www.josseybass.com

FIRST PAPERBACK EDITION PUBLISHED IN 2006.

Published by Jossey-Bass
A Wiley Imprint
989 Market Street, San Francisco, CA 94103-1741   www.josseybass.com

Scripture quotations marked "KJV" are taken from the Holy Bible, King James Version, Cambridge, 1769.

Scripture quotations marked "NCV" are taken from the New Century Version®. Copyright © 1987, 1988, 1991 by Word Publishing, a division of Thomas Nelson, Inc. Used by permission. All rights reserved.

Scripture quotations marked "NIV" are taken from the HOLY BIBLE, NEW INTERNATIONAL VERSION®. NIV®. Copyright © 1973, 1978, 1984 by International Bible Society. Used by permission of Zondervan. All rights reserved.

Scripture quotations marked "NKJV" are taken from the New King James Version. Copyright © 1982 by Thomas Nelson, Inc. Used by permission. All rights reserved.

Scripture quotations marked "NRSV" are taken from the New Revised Standard Version Bible, copyright 1989, Division of Christian Education of the National Council of the Churches of Christ in the United States of America. Used by permission. All rights reserved.

Jossey-Bass books and products are available through most bookstores. To contact Jossey-Bass directly call our Customer Care Department within the U.S. at 800-956-7739, outside the U.S. at 317-572-3986 or fax 317-572-4002.

Jossey-Bass also publishes its books in a variety of electronic formats. Some content that appears in print may not be available in electronic books.

Library of Congress Cataloging-in-Publication Data

Christian reflections on the leadership challenge / by James M. Kouzes, Barry Z. Posner, editors; foreword by John C. Maxwell.—1st ed.
　　p. cm.
Includes bibliographical references and index.
　ISBN 0-7879-6785-8 (alk. paper)
　ISBN-13 978-0-7879-8337-6 (paperback)
　ISBN-10 0-7879-8337-3 (paperback)
　1. Leadership—Religious aspects—Christianity. I. Kouzes, James M., 1945– II. Posner, Barry Z.
　BV4597.53.L43C48　2004
　253—dc22
　　　　　　　　　　　　　　　　　　　2003026456

Printed in the United States of America
FIRST EDITION
PB Printing   10 9 8 7

CONTENTS

PART 1

MODEL THE WAY

PART 2

INSPIRE A SHARED VISION

PART 3

CHALLENGE THE PROCESS

PART 4

ENABLE OTHERS TO ACT

PART 5

ENCOURAGE THE HEART

FINAL REFLECTIONS

FOREWORD

When *The Leadership Challenge* first broke out on the business publishing scene more than two decades ago, its message stood out like a beacon on a rocky shoreline. Many other business books on the market touted a "lead by intimidation" or "how to get ahead" message, providing readers with success strategies but leaving out the most important ingredient of truly inspiring leadership: a servant's heart.

Jesus has been called the greatest leader of all time, but his leadership strategy—if you could even call it that—turned conventional wisdom on its ear. You don't give to get. You give because it's the right thing to do. Want to be the greatest? Then become the servant of others. Focus on the things that matter, and the little stuff will fall into place. Don't just tell people what to do. Show them. Live by the Golden Rule, especially with those you lead. And communicate values, not through rote teaching but through stories.

Think about it. The stories Jesus told—the parables that taught such profound truths—endured through the past two thousand years, not because they listed ten action points or eight tips for leading well but because the truths he offered through these simple narratives resonate with us—real human beings—whether we go by the title of leader or learner.

In the same vein, *Christian Reflections on The Leadership Challenge* relies largely on stories to communicate the core values of its message. Though originally aimed at a general leadership market, the message of *The Leadership Challenge,* by James M. Kouzes and Barry Z. Posner, could have been lifted from the pages of scripture:

1. Model the Way
2. Inspire a Shared Vision
3. Challenge the Process
4. Enable Others to Act
5. Encourage the Heart

Each one of these Five Practices finds a parallel in the life of Jesus.

Imagine what would happen in our corporations, schools, churches, sporting associations, and private businesses if Christian leaders embodied these practices, too! When seen through the lens of a servant's heart, leadership becomes not just a job but a calling. Lives are changed for the better. Next-generation leaders are molded. Along the way, the sense of destiny God planted in each individual soul finds fulfillment.

In my speaking engagements, I remind leaders that you never truly know the potential of a person's leadership or giftedness until they lead people who don't have to follow. If you're reading these pages, you probably already knew that instinctively. You knew that the leadership gift cannot be manufactured. It can't be mustered up. It's an innate gifting that finds expression in leading the charge, bringing about change, impacting lives.

It's been said that there are two kinds of people in life: those who make things happen and those who wonder what happened. Leaders have the ability to make things happen. People who don't know how to make things happen for themselves won't know how to make things happen for others.

A leader's domain is the future, and what you do with that future means the difference between leaving a track record and leaving a legacy. That's really what *Christian Reflections on The Leadership Challenge* is all about—raising the bar on the innate leadership gift so you can incorporate The Five Practices of Exemplary Leadership® into your everyday life.

In the following pages, you'll meet diverse people of faith who faced sometimes overwhelming leadership challenges. The common denominator among them is how they lived out the Five Practices by bringing their faith to "work."

As leaders, our personal influence can be used for exciting and fulfilling results, or it can be used wrongly for disappointing results. It can be anchored by a source greater than ourselves—the wisdom of God—or it can be hampered by a self-serving motivation. The choice is up to us.

Ultimately, *Christian Reflections on The Leadership Challenge* is a book for everyone who aspires to be the best leader they can be by investing their lives in others. When men and women rise to that "Jesus pattern" of leadership, amazing things happen.

January 2004

John C. Maxwell
Founder, The INJOY Group
Duluth, Georgia

THIS BOOK

IS DEDICATED TO

OUR PARENTS

WHO WERE THE FIRST

TO TEACH US ABOUT

LOVE AND UNDERSTANDING

Christian Reflections on

LEADERSHIP
THE
CHALLENGE

1

LEADERSHIP IS EVERYONE'S BUSINESS

James M. Kouzes and Barry Z. Posner

When we began our research on leadership over twenty years ago, we were troubled by the prevailing assumption that leadership is associated with the actions of people at the top. We were troubled by the belief that leadership is something only a few people can learn and that the rest of us are doomed to leadership incompetence. We were troubled by the focus on superstar executives as *the* role models for leadership behavior.

It's not that we thought people at the top weren't supposed to be exemplary leaders. It's just that there are so few of them. The obsession with the pinnacle of power and fame left out a whole lot of people. There were certainly more exemplary leaders than the few hundred at the very apex of corporate success. We wanted to know what people from all walks of life and at all levels in the organization did to get extraordinary things done. We thought their actions were worthy of attention.

We began studying leadership one person at a time. We asked people to tell us about a time in their lives when they had been at their personal best as leaders. We asked people just like you and the people in your neighborhood. We asked men and women of all ages, races, and religions. We asked people across industries, functions, disciplines, and levels. We asked people from different geographic regions and from all over the globe. And you know what? Everyone had a story to tell, and that's still true today.

We've found exemplary leadership in churches and faith-based organizations, for-profit firms and not-for-profits, manufacturing and service organizations, governmental agencies, schools, the armed forces, health care, entertainment, and community services. Leaders reside in every city and country, in every position and place. They're employees and volunteers, young and old, rich and poor, male and female. Leadership knows no racial or religious bounds, no ethnic or cultural borders. We find exemplary leadership everywhere we look.

From our examination of these cases, as well as through the analyses of empirical data from tens of thousands of our Leadership Practices Inventories,[1] we've discovered that regardless of level, place, discipline, style, race, age, gender, religion, or personality, leaders exhibit similar behaviors when they guide others along pioneering journeys. Although each case has been unique in its expression, we've been able to detect a similar pattern to leaders' actions—a pattern we call The Five Practices of Exemplary Leadership®.[2] We've found that when performing at their best, leaders

1. Model the Way
2. Inspire a Shared Vision
3. Challenge the Process
4. Enable Others to Act
5. Encourage the Heart

The Five Practices are not the private property of the people we studied or the personal domain of a few select, shining stars. Our research challenges the myth that leadership is something inherent in the DNA or is found only at the highest levels of the organization, whether it's the executive suite or the pulpit. The theory that there are only a *few* men and women who can lead us to greatness is just plain wrong. Leadership is a process ordinary people use when they are bringing forth the best from themselves and others. *Leadership is everyone's business.* This book is about how Christian leaders apply The Five Practices to the work of mobilizing others to get extraordinary things done.

CHRISTIAN REFLECTIONS

The genesis of *Christian Reflections on The Leadership Challenge* was a request from John Maxwell to use The Five Practices as the organizing framework for the annual Catalyst Leadership Conference, sponsored by INJOY. John thought that The Five Practices provided a useful model for presenting the message of leadership to a group of energetic young Christian leaders. John also invited one of us to present at the conference. Jim Kouzes shared our framework, and his presentation received a spontaneous, enthusiastic, and joyful reception. The participants in that event could readily see that The Five Practices were as applicable to their leadership endeavors as they were to the people we'd studied in other settings.

Following Jim on the platform were six Christian leaders—Ken Blanchard, Bill Bright, John Maxwell, Kevin Myers, Nancy Ortberg, and Andy Stanley—representing legendary leadership in congregations, faith-based organizations, and secular corporations. Each shared personal stories and offered practical lessons on one of the practices. It became clear that John was right; this was a leadership framework that spoke powerfully to those in attendance.

Fueled by the enthusiastic response at the Catalyst Conference and with John's encouragement, we offered to compile a book that would make The Five Practices leadership framework speak more directly to Christian leaders, weaving together faith and leadership. Our publishers at Jossey-Bass agreed, and this book was born.

To better relate the key messages from *The Leadership Challenge* to Christian settings, we wanted to interview people from a variety of denominations who were involved in both faith-based and secular organizations. With the help of our publisher, INJOY, and our own network of colleagues, we were able to identify many exemplary leaders who'd brought Christian teachings to life and whose stories illustrated The Five Practices. We interviewed these exemplars using the same questions we had asked other leaders to find out about their personal best leadership experiences. We share their inspirational stories in Chapter Two, reviewing as we go how these leaders mobilize others to *want* to get extraordinary things done.

We also asked five recognized Christian leaders to *reflect* on The Five Practices. We asked them, "How do these practices speak to your experiences?" "What lessons do you draw from the practices that are especially applicable to Christian leadership?" "How does your faith inform your leadership?" "How can the practices help others become better leaders and better Christians?" "Based on our research and your experiences, what questions should Christian leaders ask themselves?" Their responses to these questions comprise the majority of *Christian Reflections on The Leadership Challenge.* As you'll see, these leaders speak the truth born out of firsthand experience, and they talk straight from the heart.

A FIELD GUIDE FOR LEADERS

The fundamental purpose of this book is to assist people in strengthening their abilities to lead and to make a positive difference in the world—no small aspiration to be sure, but God's work gets done most effectively when people believe they can have a positive impact. Whether you're in the role of congregant, minister, employee, manager, volunteer, parent, or student, you can apply these lessons in any setting. Whether the application is in a faith-based organization, a corporation, a governmental agency, a not-for-profit, your neighborhood, your community, or your family, this book can help you improve your capacity to guide others to places they have never been before.

We believe you are capable of developing yourself as a leader far more than tradition has ever assumed possible. It's just pure myth that only a lucky few can ever understand the intricacies of leadership. The truth is that leadership is an observable set of skills and abilities that are useful no matter where you are. And leadership, like any other skill, can be strengthened, honed, and enhanced, given the motivation and desire, the practice and feedback, and the proper role models and coaching. This book is not about being in a position (as if leadership were a place) but about having the courage and spirit to make a significant difference.

In Chapter Two, we describe The Five Practices. We provide case examples of real people who demonstrate each practice and discuss the principles underlying their actions. Through personal story and academic research, we show what leaders do when they Model, Inspire, Challenge, Enable, and Encourage.

In each of the subsequent five chapters, you find a personal reflection by a Christian leader on one of The Five Practices. In Chapter Three, John Maxwell, the impetus behind this book, reflects on Model the Way. John is founder of INJOY and Equip, as well as the author of more than twenty books, including the best-selling *The 21 Irrefutable Laws of Leadership.*[3] John tells us to "work on ourselves before we work on others" and says that "leaders' lives are mirrors, reflecting precepts they want those they lead to follow." He reminds us to be the example in the world that we want others to emulate.

David McAllister-Wilson reflects on Inspire a Shared Vision in Chapter Four. David is the president of Wesley Theological Seminary. He tells us that "Vision isn't everything, but it's the beginning of everything." David speaks to us about embracing our struggles and transforming them into an ideal future possibility.

Patrick Lencioni, in Chapter Five, reflects on Challenge the Process. Pat is president of The Table Group and the author of *The Five Temptations of a CEO*[4] and other books on leadership and teams. "Before setting out on a quest to challenge the process and change the world," he says, "Christian leaders should probably ask themselves two questions: Who am I really serving? And am I ready to suffer?" He then addresses important issues of perseverance, humility, and risk.

In Chapter Six, Nancy Ortberg reflects on Enable Others to Act. Nancy directs the Axis ministry at Willow Creek Community Church in Chicago. She tells us that "Jesus embodies the ultimate example of someone who fostered collaboration and strengthened individuals." Nancy provides very moving evidence of how giving power away is a lot more effective—and grounded in Christian principles—than grabbing and holding on to power.

Ken Blanchard reflects on Encourage the Heart in Chapter Seven. Ken's book (with Spencer Johnson), *The One Minute Manager*,[5] set in motion an entire genre of management books, and his *The One Minute Manager* library has sold more than nine million copies. Ken is also the cofounder of The Ken Blanchard Companies and now spends the majority of his time helping people learn to lead like Jesus. Caring more about others than about one's self is at the crux, explains Ken, of allowing God to work miracles through you. Ken says it's all about being a servant leader.

We think you'll appreciate the very personal nature of these chapters, as they reveal each individual's stories, struggles, and challenges. The insights from their experiences and their faith will inspire you and guide you to improving your own leadership capabilities.

As you read each of these chapters, you'll quickly realize how interdependent The Five Practices are. Although we can identify the distinctive behaviors of each practice, we also know that exemplary leadership is impossible by relying on your strength in only one. It's like expecting to be able to do the work of your entire hand by relying on only one finger. We'll pick this idea up again later.

In the closing chapter, we point out some of the common themes that weave themselves through the tapestry of these Christian reflections. We touch on the role that faith plays in the leadership process and add another observation from our research about the foundation on which all leadership practice is built. We also discuss why the first place to look for leadership is within yourself. Finally, we offer guidance about how you can continue your own growth and development.

When all is said and done, meeting the leadership challenge is a personal—and a daily—challenge. At the end of our days, the legacy we leave is the life we lead. The question that we now need to ask ourselves is, How am I going to fully use myself to make a difference in the world?

2

THE FIVE PRACTICES OF EXEMPLARY LEADERSHIP

James M. Kouzes and Barry Z. Posner

Beyond the horizon of time there is a changed world—a world different from today's world. Some people see across this boundary of experience and into the future. They believe that dreams can become realities. They open our eyes and lift our spirits. They build our trust and strengthen our relationships. They stand firm against the winds of resistance and give us courage to continue the quest. We call these people leaders. They take us to places we have never been before. We are fortunate that they do.

The Five Practices of Exemplary Leadership are not the accident of a special moment in history. They've stood the test of time. Our most recent research confirms that they're just as relevant today as they were when we first began our studies.

As you will see, The Five Practices are available to anyone—in any organization, community, congregation, or situation—who accepts the leadership challenge. To us this is inspiring. It gives us great hope for the future—hope because it means that we don't have to wait around to be saved by someone riding in on a white horse and hope because there's no shortage of potential leaders searching for the chance to make a difference. And, most assuredly in these troubling times, there is no shortage of challenging opportunities to profoundly change the world in which we live and work.

And if you're wondering if any of this really makes a difference, keep in mind that over two hundred scholars have tested The Five Practices framework in a variety of settings, including several studies of leadership in religious organizations.[1] These scholars have found that whether the setting is secular or religious, the practices are closely correlated with leadership effectiveness and member satisfaction and commitment.

LEADERS MODEL THE WAY

"Personally, I have an agenda," says Reverend Ken Horne. "There shouldn't be hungry people in the United States. It's not necessary. Therefore it is a sin to allow it, and I want that fixed. That's my agenda."

He continues: "What has always motivated me are issues of justice and issues of fairness. It's just not fair to work somebody fifty to sixty hours a week, and then he's still not able to pay his bills. Those kinds of things really jerk my chain and always have."

It's readily apparent when you listen to this plainspoken man that he cares deeply about a few key values. "If you're going to do something worth doing, you've got to be passionate about it," he says.

That agenda, passion, and caring drove Ken, in 1979, to found, along with Reverend Ray Buchanan and both their families, the Society of St. Andrew, which is located in Bedford County, Virginia. The Society of St. Andrew is a Christian ministry dedicated to meeting both spiritual and physical hungers. As their mission statement declares, "Food for the body. God's word for the spirit. Community of love for the heart. Opportunity for those who desire action." A self-described "nonleader," Ken, the executive director of the society, nonetheless has led for over two decades the food-salvage outreach program that feeds hundreds of thousands of hungry people every year.

The Society of St. Andrew wasn't what Ken started out to do. He and Ray were both in the pastorate. But as time passed, they began to realize that they didn't feel particularly called to preach. After two or three years of soul-searching prayer, Ken and Ray recognized that they were called to minister to the poor.

Their day jobs as full-time ministers, however, wouldn't allow the time needed to really make a difference to Virginia's poor and hungry. So they took a proposal to their denominational leader, got his blessing, and formed a Christian community on fifty acres of farmland, raising grass-fed beef cattle and doing odd jobs to raise money for educational retreats and workshops about ministry to the poor. "We envisioned ourselves living very simply and living on just a little," Ken told us.

During a particularly low point in their journey, the driving ministry of the Society of St. Andrew—the Potato Project—was born. While conducting a retreat on how to feed the poor, Ken got into a public discussion with a potato farmer about how much food is wasted in America—20 to 25 percent of everything grown, he insisted. Eventually, the farmer agreed that he did indeed throw out a quarter of his potato crop—the ones that didn't make it to the grocery store but were still nutritious as food.

The potato farmer agreed to donate his unmarketable produce if the society would bag and ship the potatoes to soup kitchens and food banks. Ken accepted the offer, and word spread. Soon other farmers decided to donate their unusable crops—about half a million pounds altogether. Simultaneously, the society put out a call for funds to ship the produce. Today, the Potato Project channels between forty and forty-five million pounds of potatoes each year into ministries to the poor.

Their second mission—Gleaning—sprouted from the success of the Potato Project. If so many root crops were being wasted across the country, was it not likely that crops like cabbage and tomatoes and peppers were being wasted, too? The answer was obvious. But unlike potatoes, which can be dug up and stored, the unmarketable field crops were simply left in the fields to wither. So the Society of St. Andrew took on the contemporary version of the biblical tradition of gathering crops that would otherwise be left to rot in the field. Today, the society coordinates a gleaning ministry in twenty states, enlisting about thirty thousand volunteers to handpick crops that would otherwise be wasted.

A third mission—Harvest of Hope—grew organically from the Potato Project and Gleaning. Harvest of Hope offers educational training for youth in a weeklong camp setting that provides both hands-on work (gleaning in fields) and intensive training on ministering to the poor.

In reflecting back on his quarter-century of involvement in the ministry of feeding the hungry, Ken shared this: "I think that God does things in the here and now, and what was happening (many years before) was the reflection of the fact that I'm not the greatest minister you ever saw in your life and probably wasn't intended to be. But I am pretty darn good at this. It's a matter of utilizing your own talents—what you're good at—and minimizing the necessity of dabbling in what you're not very good at."

Ken uses his talents and his principles in the grittiest sense. He never asks others to do what he himself won't do, and he's willing to get his hands dirty (literally) to help feed hungry people. "I've always been relatively unimpressed by what people say as opposed to what they do, and so being willing to lead by example is very important to me," says Ken.

Because of Ken Horne, fewer people go hungry in this country. His story demonstrates how a single individual can make a difference by being clear about what he or she values and then putting those values into practice.

Ken exemplifies the practice we call Model the Way. Exemplary leaders *find their voice by clarifying their personal values and then expressing those values in their own style.* Then they *set the example* by aligning their personal actions with shared values.

Find Your Voice

One of the consistent findings in our research is that exemplary leaders, like Ken Horne, are people with strong beliefs about matters of principle. People expect their leaders to speak out on matters of values and conscience. But how can you speak out if you don't know what's important to you? How can you show you care if you don't know what you care about? To earn and sustain personal credibility, you must be able to *find your voice by clarifying your personal values and then expressing them in your own style.* By finding your voice, you take the first step along the endless journey to becoming a leader. By constantly asking yourself what value you bring to your constituents, you'll always stay at the leading edge.

Leaders understand how important it is to be clear about the values and motivations that drive them. Sometimes it takes a while to unearth those values. For Ken it took three years of fairly constant prayer. He'd believed for a long time in fairness and justice, but before that could get translated into action, he had to put his ear to his heart and just listen.

It's essential to find your voice, because values serve as your guides. Clarity of values is essential to knowing which way, for each of us, is north, south, east, and west. The clearer we are, the easier it is to stay on the path you've chosen. Values inform your decisions about what to do and what not to do, when to say yes or when to say no, and to really understand *why* you make those decisions. They supply you with a moral compass by which to navigate the course of your daily life. This kind of guidance is especially needed in difficult and uncertain times. When there are daily challenges that can throw you off course, it's crucial that you have some signposts that tell you where you are.

It's also essential that you be able to express your values in a way that is genuinely and authentically you. You must authentically communicate your beliefs in ways that uniquely represent who you are. You must interpret the lyrics and shape them into your own singular presentation so that others recognize that you're the one who's singing the song and not someone else.

Set the Example

Clarity about personal values is an essential part of modeling the way for others. Yet leaders don't just stand up for some personal or idiosyncratic set of values. If that were true, then the only person you'd be leading would be yourself. When you're leading a group or an organization, you have to move from "what *I* believe" to "what *we* believe."

As much as we might like to, none of us can impose values from the top. A lot of people have tried that and found that it either leads to compliance or rebellion, usually the latter. Values cannot be forced. They must be forged. What being clear about personal values allows us to do is be able to detect where there are shared values in the community. Ken was not the only person who was concerned about feeding the hungry, but it was only after clearly hearing his own calling that he could then call out to others who shared his passion.

Discovering values that can be shared is the foundation for building productive and genuine working relationships. Although leaders honor the diversity of their many constituencies, they also stress their common values. Leaders build on agreement. They don't worry about getting everyone to be in accord on everything. This goal is unrealistic, perhaps even impossible.

The research is very clear that tremendous energy is generated when individual, group, and institutional values are aligned. Commitment, enthusiasm, and drive are intensified, as people have reasons for caring about their work. When individuals are able to care about what they are doing, they are more effective and satisfied. They experience less stress and tension. Shared values are the internal compasses that enable people to act independently and interdependently—simultaneously.

Yet even when *we* are clear and *we* are in agreement, we're still just talking—saying words. The Bible is full of good words; it's packed with all kinds of wisdom. But simply reading the Bible out loud doesn't make someone a credible leader. The words themselves aren't enough, no matter how noble they are. The most powerful thing a leader can do to mobilize others is to *set the example by aligning personal actions with shared values.* Leaders are measured by the consistency of their deeds and words—by walking the talk. Leaders show up, pay attention, and participate directly in the process of getting extraordinary things done. Leaders take every opportunity to show others by their own example that they're deeply committed to the values and aspirations they espouse. Leading by example is how leaders make visions and values tangible. It's how they provide the *evidence* that they're personally committed and competent.

Leaders *enact* the meaning of the organization in every decision they make and in every step they take. Leaders understand that they bring shared values to life in a variety of settings—in staff meetings, one-on-one conferences, telephone calls, e-mails, sermons, and visits with parishioners and community members.

How you spend your time is the single clearest indicator, especially to other people, about what's important to you. Critical incidents— chance occurrences, particularly at a time of stress and challenge— offer significant moments of learning for leaders and constituents. Critical incidents are often the most dramatic sources of moral lessons about what we should and should not value, about how we should and should not behave. They become stories that are passed down, whether around the workplace, in the sanctuary, or out in the community.

So you might want to try this simple process that Lillas Brown told us about. When we interviewed her, Lillas was the director of Business and Leadership Programs at the University of Saskatchewan's Extension Division. Lillas is a woman of strong faith and someone who clearly understands what she values. To stay true to her principles, at the end of every day Lillas opens her journal. "I use my journal to dialogue with the small still voice within. Every evening I ask, 'What have I done today that demonstrates this value that is near and dear to me? What have I done inadvertently to demonstrate this is not a value for me? What do I need to do to do more fully express my values?'" By daily clarifying and reaffirming her values, Lillas is able to strengthen her resolve to contribute. So will you.

LEADERS INSPIRE A SHARED VISION

John Sage and Chris Dearnley met in 1987 at an InterVarsity Christian Fellowship barbeque during their first week at the Harvard Business School. As new MBA students, they discovered that they both felt a bit out of place, and they became good friends. They also became prayer partners. Every single morning before class, John and Chris got together at a little coffee house on campus, and they prayed for about fifteen minutes.

Back then, they didn't say lofty prayers about feeding the hungry or healing the sick. Their prayer was, as John tells it, "Lord, please help us survive the first year." Not only did they survive that first year and go on to graduate, they now return to the Harvard Business School to present their own business case for other graduate students to analyze.

This was not their plan back in 1987, however. They knew they'd be lifelong friends, but they really had no idea that ten years later they'd be starting a business together. When they left Harvard, John went off to the world of high-tech marketing at Microsoft, then to a start-up with Paul Allen, one of Microsoft's founders, and then to a stint at Starbucks. Chris started out as a consultant but felt called to the ministry and started a mission in San Jose, Costa Rica, serving the poor children of that country.

Because of the bond of friendship they shared while at Harvard, John and Chris stayed in touch over the years by e-mail and telephone, and they met in person once a year. It was at one of their annual get-togethers that the dream of their company was revealed. They were sitting around talking about what was going on in their lives—John talking about his work and Chris talking about his mission in Costa Rica. Although Chris's funding for the mission was always precariously in doubt, John was constantly struck by the passion Chris had for his ministry and his outreach work. It was a counterpoint to his life in the fast lane.

At some point during their conversation, Chris pulled out a bag of Costa Rican coffee beans and presented it to John. John, who'd been working with Starbucks, knew coffee pretty well. He turned to Chris and asked him how much he had spent on it. Chris gave John one of those looks you give someone who's asked you how much a gift costs, but because they were such good friends, Chris told him it ran about $3.

John looked at the bag of beans, looked up at Chris, and said, "Well, that's about a $10 bag of coffee here in the U.S. What would happen if we created our own company, featuring coffee from your country, and used the profits from the sale of the coffee to support your work with kids? Maybe we could create a funding engine that would cover not only your current cost but help fund and propel your work?"

Without pausing a second, Chris said, "Wow! We could call it Pura Vida Coffee. 'Pura Vida' means 'pure life' in Spanish, and in Costa Rica it's colloquial for 'cool,' 'awesome,' or 'great.'" That phrase also captured the vision they had for the kids—a pure life for children in need. They stayed up most of the night envisioning the future.

The next morning, Chris took John to the airport. John was really excited. He'd been searching for something new to do, and he'd always had an interest in trying to integrate business with some kind of ministry and charitable work. He was ready to start working the phones and trying to figure out what to do to get the business launched. As they sat in the parking lot before John's flight, however, Chris suggested that they do nothing for the next thirty days except pray on the idea. That felt totally against the grain to John, but he agreed. They prayed faithfully for a month, postponing any action on the new business idea.

"And yet," says John, "in that month the way God revealed Himself and gave us direction and affirmation was striking." The company was launched. As CEO, John now handles the business side from Seattle, and Chris oversees Pura Vida Partners' mission in Costa Rica.

In the intervening years, the company has grown from nothing to a business that moves between six and eight tons of coffee a month to customers in all fifty states in the United States. They've doubled sales each of the last four years, with no signs of slowing. They specialize in the fair trade of organically grown, shade-grown coffee, so there is also a social justice and environmental stewardship to their mission. And, indeed, through their Pura Vida Partners, 100 percent of the net profits go to fund the programs that Chris leads from Costa Rica.

This is the power of a compelling vision. But it's not just the vision, as potent as it is, that has enabled John to grow the business in Seattle while Chris has cared for the kids. It's also how the vision speaks to something deeper in people. Consider the story about how John recruited Greg Forsythe, their chief financial officer. Greg was an experienced executive who'd worked at IBM, among other companies, and who'd had ten years in the coffee business. He was a perfect fit.

John and Greg hit it off. They were both committed to their faith. Greg knew everything about the coffee business, and he was a mature executive who could mentor the younger folks in the company. The only problem was that Greg was out of their league financially, and he'd been offered the number-two spot at Jiffy Lube out of Houston. There was absolutely no way that John could match the salary offer, so it appeared as if Pura Vida would be losing Greg's expertise.

John drove Greg to the airport to catch a flight for a house-hunting trip to Houston. They were sitting in the car at curbside, and Greg was about to get out of the car. John turned to Greg and said, "Just remember the Jiffy Lube slogan." Greg looked at him, a little puzzled, and John continued, "I just saw one of their ads on TV, and their tag line is 'We don't want to change the world, we just want to change your oil.'" John wished Greg good luck, and off he went.

Greg came back from that trip, having turned down the offer at Jiffy Lube, and accepted the position at Pura Vida Coffee at a fraction of the pay. In his case, it's very true that it was not about the money. It was about the meaning. John simply communicated in a very striking way how important meaning is.

Leaders like John and Chris passionately believe that they can make a difference. They have a desire to make something happen, to change the way things are, to create something that's never existed before. They have a sense of what the results will look like, even before they've started working on a project. They are driven by this clear image of what the organization can become. Leaders *inspire a shared vision.* They envision the future, and they enlist others in a common vision.

Envision the Future

Leaders *envision the future by imagining exciting and ennobling possibilities.* A vision is a mental picture of what tomorrow could be like. It expresses our highest standards and values. It sets us apart and makes us feel special. It spans years of time and keeps us focused on the future. A vision gives focus to human energy. And if it's to be attractive to more than an insignificant few, it must appeal to all who have a stake in it.

No matter what term is used—whether *vision, purpose, mission, legacy, dream, goal, calling,* or *personal agenda*—the intent is the same: leaders want to do something significant, to accomplish something that no one else has yet achieved. What that something is—the sense of meaning and purpose—has to come from within. The Pura Vida Coffee vision is a clear example of how a vision emerges out of leaders. Although their story is somewhat unusual in its epiphanous quality, it illustrates how visions flow from the inside out, not the outside in.

But just knowing that they're important doesn't make visions pop out of your head like bright light bulbs. At first glance, that may seem to be what happened with John and Chris. But take another look. Their vision for Pura Vida Coffee appeared to them *ten years after* they'd struck up a friendship. It was after many annual get-togethers in which they shared their lives. It wasn't something that came from a weekend workshop.

When we ask people to tell us where their visions come from, they often have great difficulty describing the process. And when they do provide an answer, typically it's more about a feeling, a sense, a gut reaction, or a hunch. When people first take on their roles as leaders, whether they're appointed or whether they volunteer, they often don't have a *clear* vision of the future.

At the beginning, what leaders often have is a *theme.* They have concerns, desires, hypotheses, propositions, arguments, hopes, and dreams—core concepts around which they organize their aspirations and actions. Leaders begin the process of envisioning the future by discovering their themes. Finding your vision, like finding your voice, is a process of self-exploration and self-creation. It's an intuitive, emotional process. There's often no logic to it.

Enlist Others

Having *your* vision of the future isn't enough, however. Others must be able to see themselves in that future. You can't impose your vision on others; it has to be something that has meaning to *them,* not just to you. Leaders *enlist others in a common vision by appealing to shared aspirations.* They breathe life into visions. They communicate hopes and dreams so that others clearly understand and embrace them as their own.

There is in all people a deep yearning to make a difference. We want to know that we've done something on this earth, that there's a purpose to our existence. Work can provide that purpose, and, increasingly, work is where men and women seek it. Work has become a place where people pursue meaning and identity.

Exemplary Christian leaders are able to release this human longing by communicating the meaning and significance of what people do—whether in the church, the workplace, or the community—so that they understand their own important role in creating it. When leaders clearly communicate a shared vision, they ennoble those who work on its behalf. They uplift people's spirits.

Leaders know what motivates their constituents. They forge a unity of purpose by showing constituents how the vision can meet their needs and serve the common good. In order to sense the deeper meaning and purpose people are seeking, leaders have to listen. They have to listen not just with their ears but also with their eyes and hearts. In a sense, leaders hold up a mirror and reflect back to their constituents what they most desire.

Constituents also want leaders with enthusiasm, with a bounce in their step, with a positive attitude. We follow people with a can-do attitude, not those cynics who give twenty-five reasons why something can't be done or who don't make us feel good about ourselves or what we're doing.

Enthusiasm is infectious, and people want to catch that positive energy. Energy and enthusiasm convey that we'll be part of an invigorating journey. Few will ever struggle for very long unless the experience gives them life. Leaders must fuel their constituents with hope and inspiration.

LEADERS CHALLENGE THE PROCESS

When Betty Stanley Beene became president and CEO of the United Way of America, one of the first things the staff noticed when they entered her office was a big bowl of Crayolas on her desk. Not surprisingly, everyone wondered why the national leader of a powerful charity would keep crayons at her fingertips—and theirs.

"I would tell them that when we color as adults, we color very differently than we did as children. We color more creatively; we can even color outside the lines," Betty explained. "The crayons were simply a visible reminder of the creativity that would be required of all of us to achieve the dramatic change demanded to resurrect the United Way brand."

That message of creative change was critical to Betty, who assumed the reins at the United Way of America at a time when the nonprofit was still reeling from the mismanagement and excesses of one of her predecessors, William Aramony, who had been convicted of fraud in connection with his misuse of the charity's funds.

In giving her staff the freedom to color outside the lines, Betty was sending a signal that that this was not going to be the business-as-usual environment—not for them and certainly not for her. She faced one of the toughest battles of her professional life as she implemented changes designed to transform the culture and streamline an organizational system whose relevance—and future—was clearly in question.

Betty never asked her staff to do a job that she herself was not willing to do. She had an impressive "Just do it!" track record. As a local United Way leader in Houston, she spent a night in a shelter with a homeless woman who was reluctant to stay there alone. She persuaded the top clergy of several denominations to join her on an overnight field trip to see what the homeless experienced on a regular basis. In Washington, she routinely pitched in and worked late into the night stuffing envelopes or helping out on a similar project alongside her staff.

For Betty, the unwavering rule at the core of decision making in any organization is what she calls the "sunshine test"—doing everything openly and aboveboard so as to avoid a situation like the Aramony debacle. "If it doesn't look good in the light of day, don't do it," she told United Way leaders. "If you're not going to be happy to read about it on the front page of the paper, don't do it." For Betty, there was no way changes could be made if people questioned her integrity.

Betty followed this path of openness when she took on her new role as national president and CEO of the United Way. She spent the first thirteen months traveling around the county, visiting United Way leaders in every state to learn firsthand about their successes, challenges, and opportunities. What she learned confirmed that to achieve the scale and scope of change needed in the United Way system, she would have to "break a lot of glass"—shatter the old and ineffective ways of doing things—in order to transform the United Way into an organization that was transparent and relevant. And if you're going to break a lot of glass, you know that some aren't going to like what gets shattered.

Changes were implemented smoothly at the national headquarters and with most of the fourteen hundred local United Way chapters, but, as is often the case with major change, the situation was not so pleasant in all quarters. A few of the largest local United Way chapters questioned their new national leader's publicly stated plans for change. Although most local officials welcomed the fresh air and bright light that Betty brought to the charity, a vocal but powerful minority soon discovered that the changes she was describing could threaten their personal control of local operations, if not their job security. Despite her openness, her critics charged her with working behind the scenes to centralize the charity's power at the Washington headquarters, stripping local chapters of some of their autonomy.

Still, Betty continued to take the risks she had anticipated when she signed on for the job, knowing that the changes she had to make would inevitably cost her her job. "When you have to draw that proverbial line in the sand and ask people to step on your side or the other," she said, "it's time to go." And so it happened. Eventually, some of the larger dissenting chapters withheld the dues they were required to pay to the national organization, and Betty's run as president and CEO ended with her resignation in the fifth year.

But even though her tenure was cut short, Betty had not failed. Because of the innovative strategies that had succeeded, Betty was able to leave the United Way of America in 2002, knowing that she had fulfilled the purpose of her calling. One of her most satisfying achievements extends far beyond the reach of the United Way: Betty had lobbied long and hard to have the telephone number 211 set aside for local health and human services hotlines. With the help of organized labor and a most creative and determined United Way of America staff, she eventually succeeded. The system is now operable in two dozen major cities.

"I believe so strongly that God called me to this work. When I left, I felt just as strongly that He was calling me to go," Betty said. "Faith helps you understand that you are not the work and the work is not yours. God is in charge of it all, and if you will put your trust in Him, He will enable you to do amazing things, things you never dreamt possible." When people see their work as a calling, she says, they have the tenacity to hold on during the tough times.

"If I hadn't had my faith, I absolutely could not have gotten through it," Betty said. "I never felt like I was operating alone, even in those most difficult times, when the criticism was very personal and very ugly. Time and time again, I prayed the words of the Jesus Prayer I was taught long ago, 'Lord, have mercy; come quickly to help me.' He always did."

Now a visiting scholar at Wesley Theological Seminary in Washington, D.C., Betty also leads an adult Sunday school class in her church and serves on the board of the National Alliance to End Homelessness and on the board of a Washington think tank called the Center for Strategic and International Studies—all appropriate positions for a woman who's always been one to question the accepted ways of getting a job done.

Betty Beene's story demonstrates very clearly that the work of leaders is change. Leaders don't have to change history, but they do have to change "business as usual." To them, the status quo is unacceptable. Leaders *challenge the process.* They search for opportunities, and they experiment and take risks. Exemplary leaders also know that they have to be willing to make some personal sacrifices in service of a higher purpose.

Search for Opportunities

Exemplary leaders *search for opportunities by seeking innovative ways to change, grow, and improve.* They're always on the lookout for anything that lulls a group into a false sense of security, and they constantly invite and create new initiatives that can make a difference. The focus of a leader's attention is less on the routine operations and much more on the untested and untried. Leaders are always asking, "What's new? What's next? What's better?" That's where the future is. For the sake of the future of the United Way of America, Betty Beene knew that she absolutely had to look for new ways of doing things.

People who become leaders don't always seek the challenges they face. Challenges sometimes seek leaders. But it's not so important whether you find the challenges or they find you. It's the choices you make that are crucial. Leaders must seize the initiative.

Seizing the initiative has absolutely nothing to do with position. It's about attitude and action. Innovation and excellence are the result of people at all levels making things happen. Consider the crayons and drawing pads that Betty distributed at United Way, which started popping up on conference tables, lunch tables, and almost any flat surface in the national headquarters building. No surprise, then, to say that for innovation and continuous improvement, everyone needs to believe that they can make something happen. It's the responsibility of leaders to create the environment in which "Just do it!" isn't an advertising slogan but a fact of life. Betty gave the staff the freedom to be both innovative and inquisitive. She frequently reminded them that the statement "we've always done it that way" is simply a statement of fact, not a predictor of future action. And at quarterly "All Hands Meetings," any staff member could either openly or anonymously question her about the charity's direction or her actions and receive an answer on the spot, without fear of retribution.

Leaders provide opportunities for people to exceed their previous levels of performance. They regularly set the bar higher. And the best leaders understand the importance of setting the bar at a level at which people feel they can succeed. Raise it too high, and people will fail; if they fail too often, they'll quit trying. Raise the bar a bit at a time, and eventually more and more people master the situation.

Exemplary leaders appreciate that improvements and innovations can come from just about anywhere. We know from the research that customers and frontline employees are the sources of most improvement ideas in organizations. The crayons on Betty's desk symbolized a call for creativity. And others heard it. More than likely, the best ideas for improving your local church come from members of the congregation. Consequently, leaders must be actively looking at and listening to what's going on around them for even the fuzziest sign or weakest signal that there's something new on the horizon. This means that leaders need to use their *outsight*. They must stay sensitive to the external realities.

So what motivates leaders and their constituents to seek new and innovative ways of doing things? There's an outworn cliché in business that says, "What gets rewarded gets done." There's an almost mindless acceptance that it's huge salaries, big bonuses, stock options, and lavish perks that motivate people to perform at their best, even though there is little evidence that these things get people to excel. It's just not true that people do extraordinary things because there's a tangible prize at the end.

Extrinsic motivation certainly can't explain why any of the Christian leaders we've interviewed do what they do. People don't care for the poor and the needy because they get paid huge sums of money for doing so. People don't volunteer to build homes for low-income families or seek to heal the sick because they're offered stock options. People don't treat people with dignity and respect because there's a bonus in it. You can't pay people to care. It's *not* what gets rewarded but what *is rewarding* that gets done well! Remember that Betty saw her work as a calling, not a job, and that her faith sustained her, especially during the most stressful times.

People get through the tough times—the times when they don't think they can even get up in the morning or take another step, deliver another sermon, teach another class, refurbish another inner-city home, attend another prayer meeting, organize another fund-raising drive, or hold another board meeting—because they have a strong sense of meaning and purpose. The motivation to deal with the challenges and uncertainties of life comes from the inside. It comes from finding the *work itself* rewarding. It comes when it feels like a calling and not a job.

Experiment and Take Risks

Innovation is risky. Just ask Betty Beene. New programs and projects are initially hypotheses and explorations. They are not sure things. Exemplary leaders *experiment, take risks, and learn from the accompanying mistakes.* They encourage others to step out on an adventure into the unknown rather than play it safe.

It may seem ironic, but the overall quality of work improves when people have a chance to fail. Whatever the endeavor, the "learning curve" is not a straight line. Consider the times when you tried to learn a new game or a new sport. Did you get it right the very first day? Not likely. Uncertainty, risk, and mistakes are part of the price we pay for innovation, major improvements, and, ultimately, learning.

So how do we handle the inevitable failures that accompany innovation? The most productive and supportive thing leaders can do is to create a learning climate. That kind of climate is created when leaders don't punish failure, fix blame for mistakes, or add a bunch of rules to control everything. Instead they ask, "What can be learned from the experience?"

We know that change is stressful, and every single one of the personal best leadership experiences that we collected was a difficult and demanding project. Yet each one also generated enthusiasm and joy. How can this be? How can something be both stressful *and* enjoyable? That's because it isn't stress that makes us ill; it's how we respond to stressful events. People with a hardy attitude take change, risk, turmoil, and the strains of life in stride. When they encounter a stressful event, whether positive or negative, they consider the event engaging; they feel that they can influence the outcome, and they see it as an opportunity for development. Exemplary leaders find ways to promote this kind of psychological hardiness among their constituents. Betty is a case in point. She didn't find the stress of the challenge overwhelming and debilitating. Instead, she embraced it—in fact was energized by it—and persisted in making a positive contribution.

There's another paradox in challenging the process. The dream must be grand, but the process of fulfilling the dream must be a series of small acts. We know we want to get to the mountaintop. We also know we can't get there in one big leap.

Many of today's challenges can appear overwhelming and beyond our capacity. They seem so impossible that they discourage us from even trying. Exemplary leaders break the journey down into measurable goals and milestones, demonstrating how progress can be made incrementally. Recovery, renewal, and transformation come in small improvements, not in tectonic shifts. We get there one step at a time.

LEADERS ENABLE OTHERS TO ACT

In a Sunday school class at the Mount Olivet United Methodist Church in Arlington, Virginia, one of the congregants announced that she needed a volunteer to teach that evening's ESL (English as a Second Language) class. Although Monte Campbell was new in town and knew nothing about ESL, she raised her hand. Monte was a high school teacher and said she'd be happy to be of any help she could. So she showed up that Sunday night in the church basement and, she told us, "That was the beginning of this love affair."

After a few months, because the director of the program was unable to continue, the pastor asked Monte if she'd take over. She accepted, saying she'd do what she could. The program expanded in her church, and then they started to work with a sister congregation to begin a similar ESL operation. "Before you knew it," Monte said, "the program mushroomed exponentially because the need was so great. Here I am, thirteen years later, and the program has expanded beyond our wildest dreams." Today, there are nineteen United Methodist Churches offering English classes, and in 2002 they enrolled fifteen hundred students and brought three hundred volunteer teachers into the classroom.

Because of this rapid growth and the need for outside funding, in 1995 these programs formed a board of directors and incorporated as a 501(C)3 nonprofit so they could apply for corporate and foundation dollars. ESL and Immigrant Ministries, as it's now called, acts as the umbrella organization supporting the nineteen programs. Monte serves as director.

But Monte's not the typical boss atop a pyramid. Although Monte and Mount Olivet helped to launch all the ESL programs, each of the nineteen churches has its own autonomous leadership, staff, facilities, and volunteers. Monte has no direct-line authority over any member of this "confederation and family," as she likes to call them.

So how does ESL and Immigrant Ministries get anything done? "It's an unusual arrangement," Monte admits. "I think that it's largely due to the goodwill that we share among all of us that are working together.... There just have been so many compassionate people that have shared the same sense of concern that I have shared."

Yet a collective feeling of goodwill and compassion doesn't mean there won't be disagreements. For example, from the beginning there was an understanding among the nineteen programs that there would be a modest fee to pay for services. Although all labor is volunteered, funds are needed for some operations. The initial fee was $10 per student per semester. Needless to say, with the expansion of the program, expenses grew over time. Because they weren't able to raise as much money from corporate and private contributions as they had hoped, the board felt that a modest increase in the fee was necessary—from $10 to $15 a semester. That may sound like a small amount of money, but as Monte told us, "To get that agreement among all of the programs was a formidable challenge. We weren't looking for a majority. We had to have 100 percent consensus. It was all for one and one for all. We were going to all go to $15, or none of us were going to go to $15." (From the beginning of ESL, one member organization had never charged any fee at all, so its tradition was maintained, and it was not part of the group of eighteen that had to reach unanimity.)

When you have nineteen autonomous organizations, there are bound to be some who resist a change. And some did. So what did Monte do? One thing she did was to "meet with a large number of the coordinators individually. We sat down, and I tried to listen to what they were saying and what their teachers were saying." This listening campaign, followed up by a position paper from Monte and a lot more "lobbying," eventually led to the consensus needed to raise the fee.

Monte Campbell is very humble about her role in all this. But our research tells us that it takes more than good intentions to hold together a loose confederation of independent-minded organizations. Like the other leaders in our study, Monte knows that grand dreams don't become significant realities through the actions of a single individual. Exemplary leaders *enable others to act.* They foster collaboration and strengthen individuals.

Foster Collaboration

Monte Campbell will be the first to tell you that she can't do it alone. You simply can't educate over fifteen hundred ESL students and then engage more than three hundred volunteer teachers all by yourself. The myth of the hero leader is just that—pure myth. Collaboration is the master skill that enables teams, partnerships, and other alliances to function effectively, so leaders *foster collaboration by promoting collaborative goals and building trust.*

At the very heart of cooperation is trust. Leaders help create a trusting climate by the example they set and by active listening. Trusting leaders give people the freedom to innovate and take risks. They nurture openness, involvement, personal satisfaction, and high levels of commitment to excellence.

Knowing that trust is key, leaders make sure they consider alternative viewpoints and engage people with a variety of abilities and expertise. Because they're more trusting of their groups, they're also more willing to let others exercise influence over group decisions. It's a reciprocal process. By demonstrating an openness to influence, leaders contribute to building the trust that enables their constituents to be more open to the leader's influence. Trust begets trust.

In addition, fostering collaboration can be sustained only when leaders promote a sense of mutual reliance—the feeling that we're all in this together. In any effective long-term relationship, there must be a sense of mutuality. If one partner always gives and the other always takes, the one who gives will feel taken advantage of over time, and the one who takes will feel dependent, even resentful. To develop cooperative relationships, leaders must quickly establish norms of reciprocity among partners and within teams. This kind of collaboration was absolutely essential when ESL and Immigrant Ministries faced its funding challenge.

Leaders like Monte Campbell also make sure that there's regular human contact. There has to be positive face-to-face interaction. In our new virtual world, leaders are tempted to rely more and more on electronic means of communication. Although they use the tools of the digital age, exemplary leaders make sure there are durable interactions among all constituents.

Strengthen Others

Leaders *strengthen others by sharing power and discretion*. Creating a climate in which people are involved and feel that what they are doing is important is at the core of strengthening others. It's essentially the process of turning constituents into leaders themselves—making people capable of acting on their own initiative. Leaders give people the latitude to make their own decisions and create an environment that both builds requisite capabilities and promotes a sense of self-confidence. People who experience a sense of personal accountability feel ownership for their achievements. Exemplary leaders know that they must use their own power in service of others, so they readily give their power away instead of hoarding it for themselves.

After telling us her story of gaining consensus around the increase in student fees, Monte Campbell said something that caused us to do a double take. She said, "Power sharing is dangerous." This didn't seem to fit with what she had described or with what we knew about her. We asked her what she meant. "The minute you share power, you run the risk that the group may not see it the way you see it. And you have to be agreeable to live with that eventuality. So for me as a leader, it was not without trepidation that I embarked upon this course . . . because the time might come when they don't agree with me and the direction that we need to go. . . . And so I will admit to you my vulnerability in that circumstance."

This was one of the most refreshing and honest comments we've ever heard a leader make about sharing power with others. It also illustrates why Monte has been so successful. She's willing to make herself vulnerable and to *give* her power away to others. When leaders share power with others, they're demonstrating profound trust in and respect for others' abilities. When leaders help others to grow and develop, that help is reciprocated. People who feel capable of influencing their leaders are more strongly attached to those leaders and more committed to effectively carrying out their responsibilities. They *own* their jobs and take responsibility for seeing that whatever needs to get done—or to happen—does.

LEADERS ENCOURAGE THE HEART

"My dream from the time I was in seminary had been to start a new church," recalled senior pastor, Adam Hamilton. "I had come to faith in Christ in this particular community; I went to high school here, and I heard the call to ministry here. There were no United Methodist churches in this immediate area, and I wanted to start one." Two years out of seminary, he got his wish.

After reminding the local bishop of his dream, Adam got a call from his district superintendent. "He told me, 'We're willing to send you to start this new church, but we have no land, no place for you to meet, no people, and no money. But if you really want to do it, we'd love to send you out there under those conditions.'" They also told Adam that, given the demographics of the Kansas City area where they were sending him, they thought by the year 2000 he'd have five hundred worshipers on Sundays and one thousand members.

None of this deterred Adam. He responded, "I'll do it. I'll do it tomorrow. Whenever you're ready." Adam, with his wife, LaVon, and their two young daughters, went to start the church. They were its first four members. A local funeral home director heard about the mission to start a new church in the area and offered Adam the chapel of his nearby funeral home for worship services. By the end of the first month, ninety people were attending Sunday services.

Today, the church that Adam started in 1990—United Methodist Church of the Resurrection—is 12,000 members strong, has a staff of 150, and sits on a 76-acre campus. COR, as its members most often refer to it, occupies 110,000 square feet of space, with another 176,000 square feet under construction and a total of 900,000 when the master plan is completed.

Adam will be the first to tell you that he didn't make all this happen. It was all the wonderful people of the community and the Divine support they received. But Adam has a way of leading that attracts people to his ministry. They just want to follow him because of how he makes them feel. "My job," says Adam, "is to tell inspiring stories and remind people of the driving passion for our church."

But, come to think of it, it's really those coffee mugs that got it all started. Here's how Adam tells it.

We deliver coffee mugs to every first-time visitor in our church. You come on Sunday morning, you sign in the attendance notebook, and Sunday afternoon, somebody stops by your house and delivers a coffee mug and some information and thanks you for visiting.

In the first five years, I did all that. I delivered all the coffee mugs because it was my chance to get to know all these people who were visiting.

We were probably a year-and-a-half old, and a woman visited. It was the middle of winter, and we'd had this huge snowstorm. There were about ten inches of snow on the ground, and I'm out delivering a coffee mug to her. I get to her house, walk up to the front door, and she's stunned to see me there. I said, "Hi, I just wanted to thank you for coming to church Sunday. I really would love to be your pastor."

She said, "I really enjoyed being there, but I don't think you all can be my church family."

I asked, "Why not?"

She replied, "Well, why don't you come in and I'll show you." She invited me into her house. I kicked the snow off my boots, and she took me into the living room. "I want to introduce you to my son, Matthew," she said.

Matthew had severe multiple disabilities. Then she said, "We just moved here from Texas where we attended a large church. Matthew had one-on-one care during Sunday school and one-on-one care during worship. You're such a small church, there's no way we could expect that of your congregation. We really enjoyed being there this morning, but we realize it's not realistic that you could meet our needs."

I looked at her and I said, "Ann, I will make you this promise. We will do whatever it takes to be your church family, and if you'll tell me what Matthew needs and what that program looks like, in two weeks we'll have it up and running."

She said, "Well, okay," and then she told me what he would need.

I went back to the church the next Sunday, and I told the story of Matthew. Then I said to the congregation, "Matthew's mom didn't feel like we could be her church family because we're so small. She felt she couldn't reasonably expect us to have one-on-one care in Sunday school and worship every Sunday of the year. But I told her you were the kind of people who would do whatever it takes to make a little boy like Matthew feel like he had a church home. How many of you would be willing to sign up one Sunday a month to give an hour of your time to minister with Matthew?" Of course, hands went up all over the sanctuary.

That was the beginning of our Matthew's Ministry, which now has in it thirty-five people who have multiple disabilities. They all have one-on-one care in worship and Sunday school. From that we're beginning to reach out to adults with disabilities as well as to children. It all started because there was a congregation of people who were willing to say, "We will do whatever it takes to be your church."

Adam has hundreds of stories like that. They're all stories that praise the work of his congregation, his staff, and his volunteers. Adam is always recognizing others and celebrating the COR story.

"We recognize volunteers or folks who have led efforts. Sometimes it's just through a personal thank-you note or a little card," Adam told us. "Among the staff, I have a budget set aside to be able to purchase little gifts for them and reward them—a night out for dinner, for instance, with a note saying, 'Way to go. What you did was awesome.'" Among key leaders in every ministry leader, the same process takes place.

In the areas Adam is responsible for, he'll do something special. For example, when the chair of the staff parish rotated off the committee, Adam recognized him at the big Christmas party, describing the incredible impact he'd had on the staff. Then they presented him with a really beautiful vellum page from a hymnal from the 1600s. At the bottom was an inscription with his name and a note about what he'd done. Adam loves to collect antique Bibles and Bible pages, so often he'll frame a page and present it to someone who's made a contribution.

Adam also uses his sermons to point out the good works of his parishioners. "If somebody's done something remarkable, I'll recognize him or her in my sermons as a positive example of what a Christian looks like or does," he said. "A couple of weeks ago, we recognized a person in our church who has been leading a Habitat for Humanity effort for the last seven years. He'd helped to build sixty-six Habitat houses during that period of time. At the end of the service, we presented him with a pen-and-ink drawing of the latest habitat house, and I spoke about what he had done in making this possible. It served two functions. It blessed him, and it also raised up to an entire congregation of people an example of what leadership looks like at COR. It said, 'Maybe they could be like this guy some day.'"

Our research clearly supports what Adam Hamilton says and does. We can all be like that fellow who builds sixty-six Habitat houses or the person who cares one-on-one for the Matthews of the world. And you know what? When our leaders make sure that we're recognized for it, we're just more likely to want to do it.

The climb to the top is arduous and steep. People become exhausted, frustrated, and disenchanted. The vision may be noble, and the cause may be just, but the work seems to never end. People are tempted to give up. Leaders *encourage the heart* of each constituent to carry on.

Recognize Contributions

To keep hope and determination alive, exemplary leaders *recognize contributions by showing appreciation for individual excellence.* Just as Adam Hamilton does, they use thank-you notes, smiles, awards, and public praise to demonstrate their appreciation. They love to tell stories about the achievements of others. They make others feel like winners.

Recognition for contributions, however, should not be mistaken for that glad-handing, pat-on-the-back kind of behavior that is often mistaken for encouragement. And recognition is definitely *not* the "soft stuff" that cynical managers often use as an excuse for never saying thanks to anyone.

Effective recognition is always done in the context of high expectations and clear standards. By standards we mean both goals and values (or principles). They both have to do with what's expected of us, and they are both essential to creating the conditions for positive recognition.

Successful leaders have high expectations, both of themselves and of their constituents. These expectations are powerful because they are the frames into which people fit reality. There's ample research evidence that people act in ways that are consistent with our expectations of them. If we expect others to fail, they probably will. If we expect them to succeed, they probably will. Clear expectations also give people a target to shoot for and give leaders something against which to measure performance.

Positive expectations yield positive results. They create positive images in our minds and generate other positive possibilities. Positive futures for self and others are first constructed in our minds. Unless we can see ourselves as being successful, it is very difficult to produce the behavior that leads to success. Positive images make groups more effective, relieve symptoms of illness, and enhance achievement. Seeing is believing, and the results can be life-affirming and life-enhancing.

In order to be able to give recognition in a way that is genuine and meaningful, leaders have to be out and about all the time. Wherever you are—sitting in church board meetings, volunteering in the community, visiting a friend in the hospital, attending a service, holding roundtable discussions, speaking to community groups, or just dropping by a staff member's office—you should be looking for people doing the right things and people doing things right.

And if you're clear about the standards you're looking for and you believe and expect that people will perform like winners, then you're going to notice lots of examples of people making contributions to the success of your mission and setting examples for others. Keep in mind, though, that a one-size-fits-all approach to recognition feels disingenuous, forced, and thoughtless. That's why it's so important for leaders to pay attention to the likes and dislikes of each and every individual. To make recognition personally meaningful, leaders have to get to know their constituents. By personalizing recognition, they send the message that they took the time to notice the achievement, seek out the responsible individual, and personally deliver praise in a timely manner.

When recognition is personal, you do more to tap into the motivations of each person. The reasons for active engagement in work, church, and community activities are different for different people. A personalized recognition taps into the unique drives of each person. After all, leaders get the best from others, not by building fires under people but by building the fire within them.

Celebrate Values and Victories

All over the world, in every country, in every culture, people celebrate. We stop working on certain days during the year to honor historic events and pay homage to people who've made a difference in our lives. We hold impromptu ceremonies in the office to rejoice in the birth of a new baby or the crossing of a personal milestone. We attend banquets to show our respect for individuals and groups who've accomplished an extraordinary feat. We gather at the end of a grueling community project and give each other high-fives for a job well done. We attend church services to celebrate the wonder of God. And in tragic times, we come together in remembrance and song to reaffirm our common humanity.

Why do we take time away from working to come together, tell stories, and raise our spirits? Sure, we all need a break from the pace and intensity of our jobs, but celebrations aren't trivial excuses to goof off. Celebrations are among the most significant ways we have to proclaim our respect and gratitude, to renew our sense of community, and to remind ourselves of the values and history that bind us together. *Leaders celebrate the values and the victories by creating a spirit of community.* Celebrating values and victories reinforces the fact that extraordinary performance is the result of many people's efforts. By celebrating people's accomplishments visibly, leaders create and sustain team spirit. Public celebrations let everyone know that "we're all in this together." By basing public celebrations on the consistency with key values and the attainment of milestones, they sustain people's focus.

Ceremonies and celebrations are also opportunities to build healthier groups. They enable members of the organization to know and care about each other. And supportive relationships at work, at home, at church, at school, and in the community—relationships characterized by a genuine belief in and advocacy for the interests of others—are critically important to maintaining personal and organizational vitality.

Strong human connections produce spectacular results. Our studies confirm that extraordinary accomplishments are achieved when leader and constituents alike get personally involved with the task and with other people. When people feel a strong sense of affiliation and attachment to their colleagues, they're much more likely to have a higher sense of personal well-being, to feel more committed to the organization, and to perform at higher levels. When they feel distant and detached, they're unlikely to get much of anything accomplished.

Wherever you find a strong culture built around strong values, you'll also find endless examples of leaders who personally live the values. The only way to truly show people you care and that you appreciate their efforts is to be out there with them. Because leadership is a relationship, people are much more likely to enlist in initiatives led by those with whom they feel a personal affiliation. It's precisely the human connection between leaders and constituents that ensures more commitment and more support. Saying thank you—and genuinely meaning it—is a very concrete way of showing respect and enhancing personal credibility.

These Five Practices—Model, Inspire, Challenge, Enable, and Encourage—are the ways that leaders mobilize others to want to get extraordinary things done in organizations. They are the practices leaders use to transform values into actions, visions into realities, obstacles into innovations, separateness into solidarity, and risks into rewards. They are what leaders do to create the climate in which people turn challenging opportunities into remarkable successes.

Certainly, there are no shortages of challenging opportunities for Christian leaders today. In these extraordinary times, the challenges just seem to be increasing, and through our responses we have the potential to profoundly change the world in which we live, work, and worship. In the following five chapters, you'll read the reflections of five Christian leaders on how these Five Practices have impacted their own thinking and action, as well as their thoughts about the implications for other Christian leaders.

THE FIVE PRACTICES AND TEN COMMITMENTS OF LEADERSHIP

PRACTICE	COMMITMENT

Model the Way

1. Find your voice by clarifying your personal values.
2. Set the example by aligning actions with shared values.

Inspire a Shared Vision

3. Envision the future by imagining exciting and ennobling possibilities.
4. Enlist others in a common vision by appealing to shared aspirations.

Challenge the Process

5. Search for opportunities by seeking innovative ways to change, grow, and improve.
6. Experiment and take risks by constantly generating small wins and learning from mistakes.

Enable Others to Act

7. Foster collaboration by promoting cooperative goals and building trust.
8. Strengthen others by sharing power and discretion.

Encourage the Heart

9. Recognize contributions by showing appreciation for individual excellence.
10. Celebrate the values and victories by creating a spirit of community.

Source: The Leadership Challenge by James M. Kouzes and Barry Z. Posner. Copyright © 2002.

PART ONE

Model the Way

Exemplary leaders stand for something, believe in something, and care about something. They *find their voice* by clarifying their personal values and then expressing those values in their own unique and authentic style. Leaders also know they cannot force their views on others. Instead, they work tirelessly to forge consensus around a set of common principles.

Eloquent speeches about admirable beliefs, however, aren't nearly enough. Words and deeds must be consistent for leaders to have integrity. Leaders must *set the example* by aligning their personal actions with shared values. When constituents know that their leaders have the courage of convictions, they are more willing to commit. People first follow the person, then the plan.

3

REFLECTIONS ON MODEL THE WAY

John C. Maxwell

Remember your leaders, who spoke the word of God

to you. Consider the outcome of their way of life

and imitate their faith.

Hebrews 13:7, NIV

The man of integrity walks securely.

Proverbs 10:9, NIV

You've heard it over and over again: "Actions speak louder than words." If you were privileged to grow up in an environment of encouragement, count your blessings. The harsh reality, however, is that many Christian leaders today began life under less than ideal circumstances. Broken homes, absentee parents, crumbling morals in an increasingly decadent society—all these conditions factor into the making of a human being, for better or worse. Regardless of their past, God still calls men and women to serve Him in leadership roles. Even a cursory glance through the scriptures demonstrates that God specializes in taking broken, weak individuals and changing the course of history through them. He provides a clue as to why He uses this peculiar tactic in 2 Corinthians 12:9, which says, "My power is made perfect in weakness."

Many of us feel like top-notch candidates for the "weakness" category, but consider that good news. We're in a great starting position as we seek to Model the Way for others to follow. But how does one go about the task of modeling the way? Admittedly, it's a scary thought: *Others will be watching my every move and emulating what they see.* For some leaders, this concept becomes an ego trip. But every godly leader interviewed for this book was humbled by the knowledge that his or her life is a mirror, reflecting precepts for constituents to follow.

I've identified five principles that can serve as signposts as you strive to model the way:

1. Work on yourself before you work on others.
2. Work on yourself more than you work on others.
3. It is easier to teach what is right than to do what is right.
4. People do what they see.
5. The example of others profoundly impacts our lives.

FIRST LEAD YOURSELF

The first two principles go hand-in-hand, so let's examine them together.

- *Work on yourself before you work on others.*

- *Work on yourself more than you work on others.*

Of all the values that go into making a good leader, the one that scores the highest with me is following the Golden Rule. As a leader, the first person I should lead is me. If I wouldn't follow myself, why should anyone else? So therefore I have to be satisfied with leading "me." This is not a selfish motive; it's something that keeps me making sure that what I'm sharing with others and asking others to do, I'm also doing myself. If leaders don't take that inner journey to develop themselves as people, two things could happen: either they become shallow as leaders or they peter out in a very short time.

As a leader, it's imperative that you lead yourself before you lead others. This is a simple but profound truth, and often we learn it the hard way. Before we try to straighten others out, we must straighten ourselves out. It's like this conversation between Charlie Brown and Lucy:

> *Lucy:* Charlie Brown, I think I want to change the world.
> *Charlie Brown:* Well, Lucy, that's awesome. Whom would you start with?
> *Lucy:* You, Charlie Brown. I would change you first.

Many times as leaders we want to change people. But in the area of modeling the way, this principle is crucial: *Don't try to change someone else until you change yourself.* It's tempting to think leaders always lobby for change and followers dig in their heels and resist, but the truth is that leaders don't like change any more than followers—unless it's their idea. In fact, leaders *resist* change more than followers (again, unless it's their idea). Why? Because when change occurs in an organization, the first question a department leader asks is, "How is this going to affect my turf and my people?" Every time an organization ceases to change, it's because a leader got in the way. Followers never stop an organization from changing; leaders always do.

Someone asked me the other day, "Who is the first person I ought to lead?" The answer was easy. "Yourself," I told him. "In fact, that's the first person you *want* to lead. If you wouldn't follow yourself, why should anyone else?"

Change always starts on the inside. Don't try to build something great out in the world until you've tried to build something great inside. Similarly, don't worry about where you're going until you know who you are. Settle the inside issues first. When they're in order, you can start to work on the outside.

When I was a young leader working at my second church, I underwent a time of profound personal growth in which God hammered this truth into my life. It all began after I learned how to share my faith with others. It seems odd that a pastor would have to learn how to talk about his faith, but I didn't know how to do this. I knew how to preach. I knew how to give an invitation. But I didn't know how to share my faith one-on-one. I got so excited I planned an outreach night. Now I could share my newfound evangelism tactics with the congregation! I stood in the pulpit and declared, "Thursday night will be the outreach night, and at 7:00 we'll all pray together, then go out and share our faith." When Thursday night arrived, I drove to the church and unlocked the doors to the auditorium. Nobody came.

Disappointed, I went to the altar and prayed. Feeling a little humbled, I went out and shared my faith alone. The next Sunday I made a similar announcement, but Thursday night came and went and still no one showed up. In the third week, God started speaking to me: "John, don't work on the people. Work on yourself. You just do what I've asked you to do, and do it consistently. Leave all the results up to me." For nine months I unlocked the doors of the church, prayed at the altar, and went out to share my faith. And for nine months no one came.

Looking back, it's easy to see what God was up to. He was shaping me. That experience taught me that leadership is all about being the right person before you start doing the right thing. It taught me that people do follow what they see, and if I would just model it long enough they would begin to catch on. They had never seen anyone share their faith before.

As a leader, you are the picture and the model. People don't buy into your vision; they buy into you. The only way you can ever get them to buy into you with conviction and credibility is to live it first.

VALUES ARE GUIDES

Michael Joseph, chairman and CEO of Dacor—a manufacturer of high-end kitchen appliances—is one of those leaders who decided to work on himself first, and it profoundly changed the way his company does business.

In 1997, Michael decided to do something radical with the company his parents had founded three decades earlier and that he had been leading for over twenty-five years. Already a successful business, Dacor was run by ethical standards and had a reputation for quality workmanship. But Michael wanted it to be known for something more.

By the time the mid-nineties arrived, Michael's own spiritual journey had picked up speed, and he became convinced he needed to bring his faith to the workplace. Michael, who considers the "redprint portions of scripture"—the words of Jesus—to be his instruction manual for godly leadership, wanted to infuse this passion into the company.

"We already had a very nurturing environment at Dacor, but one day I took a second look at our company values statement," he recalls. "To honor God in all that we do" was part of the statement, but it was one of a series of equally weighted goals. "The more I looked at that statement, the more I realized there was really only one message that mattered; the others were just how-to statements." Michael decided to risk industry sneers—and a few raised eyebrows from his own staff of six hundred employees—to change the wording to read: "To honor God in all that we do by respecting others, by doing good work, by helping others, by forgiving others, by giving thanks, and by celebrating our lives."

Wanting to be bold about his company's new creed, Michael posted it on the Dacor Web site and printed up new business cards and marketing literature to reflect the change. As he introduced the statement to his employees, who represented twenty-six different nationalities and all major religions, he told them they were all welcome at his company. Then he added these words: "This value statement is a challenge to me personally to be a better person, and I believe it calls the company to a higher purpose. I believe that when we respect and help one another, we are able to recognize the talent throughout the organization. When we practice forgiveness and give thanks to one another, and thanks to God as well, we open and improve communications. When we deliver innovative and high-quality products, we do good work. And when our business behavior is driven by these values everyone benefits and we have many reasons to celebrate our lives."

What happened afterward was "heartwarming and overwhelmingly positive," Michael recalls. The company, including Dacor's advisory board, rallied around the new credo, connecting the employees in a way he could not have anticipated. "After the first few months of 'where's he going with this?' the people responded with gratitude. We had an outside sales force of seventy people who had this on their business cards. They were out there in the real world, on the firing line, handing these cards out. We wondered what the market's response would be. We did get a couple of derogatory comments early on, but now, several years later, it is so ingrained in the company. When a leader steps out like this it is very helpful to be surrounded by people who support him."

As a Christian whose "mission field" is the manufacturing industry, Michael considers the company creed his way of sowing spiritual seeds. "I knew I had to call the company to a higher purpose," he says. "There's a lot to be said for hard work, making good choices, and hiring good people, but then there are those things that I call divine intervention. Since I'm not a member of the clergy, the way I could give thanks and honor God's presence in my life was through this statement. I could not *not* do it."

• It is easier to teach what is right than to do what is right.

Saying you believe in Christian principles is one thing; living them every day is another, whether you lead in a business environment, like Michael Joseph, or in a ministry. As a young leader pastoring my first church, this was my first leadership challenge. I can still remember being in my first church and teaching the congregation verse by verse for several months until I came to a passage of scripture I didn't live.

The internal struggle grew intense. I began to ask myself, "What do I do with a passage of scripture I am called to teach if I'm not living up to it myself? How do I exhort other people to follow a teaching if I fall short of it myself?" This created quite a dilemma for me.

Unfortunately, I tried to wing it. After I preached that message, I made a very important decision I hold to this day: *If I don't live it, I won't teach it. I won't try to export what I don't possess.* As leaders, we teach what we know but we reproduce what we are. That revelation was huge for me.

Years ago, I picked up a book by Fred Smith called *Learning to Lead* (which is no longer in print). This simple book contained profound insights on leadership. I was on a plane from San Diego en route to a conference where I was scheduled to speak. As I turned a page into one of the chapters, the first statement leaped off the page at me: "Leadership . . . is both something you are and something you do." In other words, leadership is not just something you live but something you behave. Leadership has to be fleshed out by action. I stopped right there. I couldn't read any further. I took out a pen and made three columns on the blank facing page. The first column listed what I am, the middle column listed what I do, and the right-hand column tallied the results. I began to equate the fact that what I am and what I do have to match up. I can't be somebody my behavior doesn't reflect. As the truth of this reality settled over me, I knew I had to become a model that others could follow. One of the words I wrote down was *character,* so the columns read something like this: "If I am a person of character (left-hand column), I will do what is right (middle column). And if I do what is right, the result is that I'll have credibility (right-hand column)." I went through this exercise with several different leadership traits. When what I am and what I do match up, I have both character and credibility. If they don't match up, I'm in trouble as a leader.

So keep our starting principle in mind: *It is easier to teach what is right than to do what is right.* Powerful leadership emerges when your life matches the message. Michael Joseph knows this all too well. "Words are important, but they're not important if you don't behave consistently. For one thing, nobody's going to believe you and follow you. The challenge for Christian leaders is to take the first step, no matter what that step is. Effective leaders convey their message through their behavior and actions, not just through their words." So Michael and the other Dacor leaders had better practice what they preach during the good times and especially during the bad.

Perhaps the most surprising show of support from Dacor leadership for its values came during the economic downturn of 2002. Like most other businesses, Dacor experienced a financial setback and was forced to cut back overtime during the third quarter. To an hourly employee, losing those extra hours at time-and-a-half pay had a serious economic impact, and Michael knew it. He responded by raising the factory workers' base pay 10 percent, a move that cost the company an additional $1 million annually. Despite the recession, sales grew 22 percent in 2002, and profit jumped 40 percent from previous years. Remarkably, in the past four years—years that followed the adoption of the new company creed—Dacor's annual sales have doubled, from $100 million to $200 million.

"There are other small things we do, like birthday cards and sitting down with every person who joins the company, whether they're a spot-loader or an executive," Michael says. "I take the time to spend fifteen or twenty minutes with everybody who comes into the company. It's what I can do to let them know they are appreciated." Employees who don't make the grade are given what Michael calls "a soft landing" to help them get back on their feet. Dacor also provides an outside psychology hotline for employees facing family difficulties—a gesture to recognize that they have whole lives. "We're a lot more than what we do for a living. This environment demonstrates that management cares and is listening." The company also shares 10 percent of its profits with employees, as well as partial ownership.

• *People do what they see.*

This is one of the greatest motivational factors in the world. All our life, we truly do play "follow the leader," and Stanford University research indicates that 89 percent of how we learn is visual, 10 percent is aural, and 1 percent is obtained through the other senses. That's why the Apostle Paul said eleven different times in his letters to the early church, "Remember how I acted," or "Remember what I did," or "Remember what I said when I was with you." He constantly referred back to his behavior, basically telling his followers, "I know you can't always remember what I said, but you do remember what I did." This is because human beings are primarily visual learners. When you as a leader look at your people, it's like looking in the mirror because they become just like you.

In my book *The 21 Irrefutable Laws of Leadership*, I mention the law of magnetism, which states that we attract who we are, not who we want. This is an important distinction for leaders to remember: people do what they see. They hear your message, but they'll follow your footsteps.

Walt Griffin is a leader who talks with his feet. When Walt took over as principal of Lakeview Middle School in Seminole County, Florida, that school was not the type of place local parents wanted *their* children to attend. Plagued by discipline problems and rundown facilities, the school's lower socioeconomic status only made its image worse. As a result, the school failed to enroll many of the students who lived within its attendance boundary.

In addition, a representative from the U.S. Justice Department had come to Seminole County a few years earlier to examine public schools as part of a broad desegregation effort. Authorities weren't surprised at what they found. Major discrepancies existed between Lakeview and other area middle schools, which claimed a higher socioeconomic status, smaller African American population, more resources, and better opportunities. So they took action. To help make the schools more equal, authorities decided to make Lakeview a *magnet* school—the term used for select schools that focus on specific educational programs such as science, math, or liberal arts—in an effort to attract students who otherwise might not attend.

Declared a "fine and performing arts/communication magnet school" with a pre-IB (international baccalaureate) preparatory program, Lakeview needed a strong leader to turn it around and make the magnet program work. The proposed new school looked good on paper. But how do you transfer those ideals from paper to real-life practice? Could it even be done? That's where Walt comes in.

The school board transferred Walt, then assistant principal of another middle school, to serve as Lakeview's assistant principal and to coordinate the magnet program. Known for his tireless work ethic and contagious enthusiasm, he caught the vision for the "new" school and set to work bringing it into fruition.

"It was a huge task and a fascinating experience for me," says Walt, who points out that although faith is an integral part of his value structure, he lets his actions speak for him—and loudly they do speak. "As a school leader, every action you make and word you speak is listened to by many more people than you realize, especially children," he says. "Trust, integrity, and honesty are important things for all adults to model for children. They're not the type of values you can teach through a book. Children learn by observing actions."

"I share my personal creed with the staff, but you can't just say it, you have to do it," says Walt, who has fostered an environment of concern for the "whole person" at Millennium (the name change reflects the transformation of this magnet school). "They know if there's a problem I can help them with, I will. Some of our teachers have had to deal with things like divorce, death, cancer, parents going into nursing homes. We have a very strong support mechanism at the school. It's not just saying we are here for you, but somebody stopping by their house every night and finding out what they need. Those teachers are better in front of the children because they feel safe and supported here."

Walt takes his personal creed a step further, namely through the underprivileged students he takes under his wing every school year. "I select about five of the most difficult children on campus and ask them to help me in special ways. We deliver food to the needy and clothes to the poor. These are at-risk kids, who could go either way down the path. We give them anything they need, down to clothing and making sure they get breakfast every morning at school. Other kids see me with these kids all the time. It's a three-year process. We start in sixth grade, and by the time they get to high school they have all the tools they need to be successful in school."

The metamorphosis of Lakeview Middle into Millennium Middle School was a staggering success. Of the school's 1,760 students in 2002-03, 280 lived outside its attendance zone but applied to go there. That same year, the school quickly filled all its out-of-zone spots, with more than 200 children on a waiting list.

- *The example of others profoundly impacts our lives.*

Who we are today is largely a result of the input we've received over the years. Jim Kouzes and Barry Posner encourage standout leaders to "listen to the masters." They observe that, "The internal exploration of our own inner territory to find our voice is often facilitated by listening carefully to the leaders we most respect. The leaders we personally admire are rich sources of information about our own values and beliefs. We chose them for a reason, so thinking more consciously about them can be extremely insightful."[1]

Who has had a profound impact on your life? The name that tops the list for me—indeed, the man who has changed my life—is Bill Bright, founder of Campus Crusade for Christ. A couple of years ago, I wrote him a letter to express my gratitude for his example. In addition to my father, Bill has had the greatest influence on my spiritual life, and when I think of a godly leader, I think of those two.

Bill has taught me a lot about faith in God. One time when we were together in San Diego, I asked him how he became a great man of faith. I will never forget his response: "John, I study the attributes of God, and that nurtures and builds my faith." From that day on, I have followed his practice of building faith by studying the attributes of God.

Bill has also modeled for me how to seek first God's kingdom and allow other things to fall in place. I know of no one who lives this life better than he does. The leadership expression "You have to give up to go up" is a testimony of his ministry. His passion for souls and commitment to fulfill the Great Commission has fueled my heart. He is a leader of leaders, and I believe that thousands will carry on his vision. As a result, millions will come to Christ. His greatest gift to the church is the leaders he has inspired and left to carry on his life's work.

But perhaps the greatest deposit he has made in my life is his personal interest in me. Because of his love and example, I endeavor to raise my faith, vision, and passion for God; I endeavor to seek first His kingdom and raise up another generation of Christian leaders; I endeavor to pass these values and priorities on to the men and women of the INJOY leadership group. Bill modeled the way in his own life, giving me a standard to strive for.

As you seek to model the way for others, remember that your life is a beacon, not just to those you lead but to a watching world. We live in a day when corporate greed and corrupt leadership make headline news. Abuses of spiritual leadership have soured many people on the claims of the gospel. I can't think of another time in history when we were more in need of upright standards—and standard-bearers—to lead the way.

Questions for Reflection

1. Who are my leadership role models? Why do I consider them role models?
2. How clear am I about the values that guide my life and leadership?
3. How much agreement is there on values in the group I lead?
4. How aligned is the way I'm spending my time each week with my most important values?
5. How much do I talk with others about my values? How effective am I at telling stories to teach important lessons?

PART TWO

INSPIRE A SHARED VISION

There is no freeway to the future. No paved highway from here to tomorrow. There is only wilderness. Only uncertain terrain. There are no roadmaps. No signposts. Pioneering leaders rely on a compass and a dream.

Leaders *envision the future* by imagining exciting and ennobling possibilities. They dream of what might be, and they passionately believe that they can make a positive difference.

But visions seen only by the leader are insufficient to mobilize and energize. Leaders *enlist others* in exciting possibilities by appealing to shared aspirations. They breathe life into ideal and unique images of the future and get others to see how their own dreams can be realized by embracing a common vision.

4 REFLECTIONS ON INSPIRE A SHARED VISION

David McAllister-Wilson

And it shall come to pass in the last days, saith God; I will pour out my Spirit upon all flesh: and your sons and your daughters shall prophesy, and your young men shall see visions, and your old men shall dream dreams.

Acts 2:17, KJV

Where there is no vision, the people perish.

Proverbs 29:18, KJV

When I got my first job in seminary administration, I knew we had to figure out what "leadership" was. Wesley Theological Seminary was a struggling institution in the middle of Mainline Protestantism—a movement that has been declining for over a generation. I began to read those books on secular leadership you find in airport bookstores (including the first edition of *The Leadership Challenge*) for transferable concepts to save our institution and help our students become effective leaders.

I found myself looking in a mirror because these business experts were using our words! Successful entrepreneurs are called *prophets*. Good managers practice *stewardship*. Turnaround experts are *saviors*, who speak of *mission, spirit,* and *charisma*.

It isn't just coincidence. The language and the concepts of the Christian church are part of the deeply embedded operating system of Western capitalism. Indeed, the very idea of the "corporation" in law comes from us. The root word is Latin, *corpus,* meaning "body." The church is the Body of Christ, the Corpus Christi—many who are one. The church is the first and oldest corporation. We should know something about leadership. And of all the practices we should be able to teach, perhaps the most important is the one Jim Kouzes and Barry Posner call Inspire a Shared Vision.

Vision isn't everything, but it's the beginning of everything. In the words of the Proverbs 29, "without vision, the people perish." Christianity (and our parent, Judaism) is a vision about both the present and the future, and that vision is the Kingdom of God. And the way Christian leadership inspires a shared vision of the Kingdom is a model for the way leaders who are Christian can develop their own leadership.

INSPIRATION AND VISION EMERGE FROM SUFFERING

Christian leaders draw from those times in the past when things were the toughest to find themes that will speak to the current crisis. We speak of light and dark, lost and found, slavery and freedom, sin and salvation; we speak of the Mount of Zion and the valley of the shadow of death. We draw on the biographies of biblical figures and the saints of the church as role models.

Think of the prophet Jeremiah. Israel had lost everything, Jerusalem was destroyed, and the Israelites were kicked out of the promised land. In chapter 33, God said to Jeremiah, "Call me, Jeremiah, and I will show you things you have not seen." Neither is it accidental that in the uncertain and disquieting times in which we now live, people seek more spiritual guidance. The promise that hope emerges from suffering is one of the unique contributions of our faith.

Listen to the last lines of the last sermon Martin Luther King Jr. preached on the night before he was killed:

"Well, I don't know what will happen now. We've got some difficult days ahead. But it doesn't matter with me now. Because I've been to the mountaintop. And I don't mind. Like anybody, I would like to live a long life. Longevity has its place. But I'm not concerned about that now. I just want to do God's will. And He's allowed me to go up to the mountain. And I've looked over. And I've seen the Promised Land. I may not get there with you. But I want you to know tonight, that we, as a people will get to the Promised Land."[1]

For those of us raised in the church, he was talking to us in the code of the Jews and the Christians. When he spoke of seeing the promised land, all of us Sunday school kids knew what he was talking about. He was giving us a hyperlink to the story of Moses, who leads the people out of slavery, into the wilderness, finally to the banks of the river Jordan, ready to cross into the land promised to Abraham and his descendants. Moses did not live long enough to cross into the promised land, but he was able to look over and see it from the top of a mountain.

As the scriptures unfold, the promised land and its capital, Jerusalem (also called Zion), represents hope for the future, the fulfillment of God's promise to gather all His lost children and bring them home. Whenever we sing of "Zion" or when we pray, "thy kingdom come," that's what we're talking about; that's what we're hoping for.

A deep understanding of the Christian faith infuses leaders with hope. We come to realize that if we take the time to look over the horizon, we will see a better tomorrow.

VISIONS HAVE A RAINBOW QUALITY

We often say, "Seeing is believing." But the deeper truth is that believing is a certain way of seeing. Ask anyone who has accomplished something great, and they will tell you that first came the vision.

Bill Shore, founder of the Share Our Strength Foundation, calls these visions "the cathedrals within."[2] It took a whole region, thousands of people, and several generations to build one of those great cathedrals. What produced that sense of mission was a grand vision. The great cathedrals are in the shape of a cross, and their spires were meant to look from a distance like the silhouette of the heavenly city rising in the medieval sky.

Christian leaders believe in the power of the vision to renew institutions. Beecher Hicks is the pastor of Metropolitan Baptist Church in Washington, D.C., one of the city's great institutions. But Pastor Hicks decided he needed to "get the church out of the church" in order to be a witness to the city. So he planned to hold Easter services on the grounds of the Washington Monument.

It took months of preparation and about $40,000 to set up the giant tent, thousands of chairs, the outdoor propane heaters, the electric system for the lights and sound, and the remote television cameras and monitors. The church raised the money $5 at a time, pledged by members on a weekly basis. Then the weather turned cold on Good Friday, and it snowed Saturday night. Come Sunday, it had stopped snowing, but it was very cold and overcast and an hour before the service, few people had arrived. But by the time Hicks rose in the pulpit, all the chairs were full. And in the middle of the service, the clouds parted and the sun came out. It got so warm, they turned off the heaters and lifted the sides of the tents, and the people on the streets of Washington—the homeless, the tourists, and the roller-bladers—all crowded around the tent as over five thousand people experienced the Resurrection that day. That kind of bold move is what has made Metropolitan a great institution in Washington.[3]

Pastors like Beecher Hicks and Christian leaders like Millard and Linda Fuller of Habitat for Humanity and Bill McCartney of Promise Keepers inspire me because they take on something big. And one of the lessons I have learned is to aim high, allowing for wind and elevation. Visions are necessarily hyperbolic, unrealistic, and irresponsible. They express goals that have a rainbow quality.

Learn to tell your story as an epic tale. Practice telling your story as an exciting adventure, and use the archetypal themes of being lost and found, of being in light and dark. Put yourself in the story in the form of an epic character from the Bible or other sources. Leave it open at the end, like it is the first or second episode of the *Lord of the Rings* trilogy.

Understanding our story in epic terms is like the very small church near my home in the poor part of town that has a sign out front advertising that "the Kingdom of God is being built here." At Wesley, in order to find the way out of the malaise of Mainline Protestantism, we have adopted the vision that "we will play a key role in the revitalization of the church." I know we cannot, but I believe we will, and this audacious belief will take us farther toward that vision than we would otherwise go.

As a Christian, your leadership will begin and end with your faith. Sometimes it is appropriate to be very open about your faith; sometimes it isn't. But you can draw on its strength as an example of visionary leadership. You know that in the end, what matters is not your personal success or the success of your organization. Put the future in God's hands, and you will be the kind of nonanxious presence people will look to for comfort and hope.

FISH WITH A NET

The ability of a leader to articulate a bold vision is only half of what it takes to practice a leadership that inspires a *shared* vision. Christianity is a group activity. We are the people of God, the tribe of Abraham and Moses, the descendants of the twelve disciples on a spiritual journey to the promised land. The *church* is a plural noun, and Christian leadership is like fishing with a net or being a shepherd of a flock; it is about gathering people together and enlisting them in a movement toward a shared vision.

Articulating this shared vision isn't all about preaching. I didn't think I would ever say that because preaching is so important, but preaching alone is ineffective and can be dangerous to the soul. Preachers can often spend their whole ministry in the pulpit, casting their thoughts in front of them like a golfer hitting into a fog bank, having no idea whether their ideas are on-target. They can come to think that they are themselves the source of divine wisdom, substituting their vision for God's. That's why in the secular world when an ineffective leader delivers a one-way, top-down harangue, it is referred to as "preaching."

Moses stuttered, and Paul considered himself unskilled in public speaking. George Whitfield was a better preacher than John Wesley, but Wesley produced a successful and enduring movement while Whitfield's oratory died with him. Successful churches, organizations, and communities are more like choirs than soloists. Christian leadership is the ability to encourage everyone to sing off the same page.

John Derrick is chairman of PepcoHoldings, Inc., and former CEO of Potomac Electric Power Company. He is one of the most successful visionary leaders I know, even though his work has always been in a highly regulated and constrained environment. And he has taught Sunday school all his life. PEPCO employees have a high degree of ownership in the company's mission. In the words of the corporate slogan, "We are connected to you by more than power lines."® John is a quiet leader, and he demonstrated the practice of sharing a vision during a severe snowstorm in Washington, D.C., in 1993. The mayor shut down all government offices and called on all employers in the District of Columbia to release all "nonessential" personnel. John made his way through the snow to faithfully attend a meeting at the Seminary that morning, and I asked him how many employees he was releasing. He was a little miffed with the question. Everyone was given the opportunity to go home if they needed to. But he said, "I will not send the message to the people who work at PEPCO that anyone is 'nonessential.'" I think he teaches that message in Sunday school, too.

My wife, Drema, is pastor of a church located two exits down the highway from the Pentagon. On the evening of September 11, she held a prayer service and people came to church, as they did all over the country, looking for spiritual leadership. They came to hear the promise of deliverance. Everyone was afraid and angry and confused. Some had been injured, and many had friends and coworkers who were killed or missing. It was like a flood of emotion, and Drema was like the Army Corps of Engineers, gently helping the torrent find its way safely back to the sea.

She didn't preach at all. Instead, she led in the flow by drawing from our common vision. She read the ancient scripture passages that spoke of comfort and hope; she selected old hymns about triumph over death, and she guided our prayers. And then, she offered time for spontaneous prayers. People prayed for those killed or still missing, for family members, for firefighters, for the country.

And then, we heard the voice of our lay leader, Brian Murray. Brian is a U.S. Army officer who had lost friends hours earlier. He asked for forgiveness of the enemy.[4] In these prayers, I heard the sound of a shared vision, for they were all really praying for the same thing out of the same hope, captured in the Lord's Prayer with the words "thy Kingdom come, thy will be done." They left the church that night with a vision and the calm courage that comes with it.

Visions like that may be harvested in crisis—what we call the "prophetic moments"—but they are planted in the other seasons of the church. The sermon is not the sole opportunity to foster vision any more than is the big speech at the stockholder's meeting, the pep talk at the annual staff picnic, or the memo attached to the quarterly profit report. How Christian leaders plant the vision is key to the practice of inspiring a shared vision.

KEEP YOUR EYE ON THE HORIZON

The question I hear so often from frustrated designated leaders is, "How can I get things going?" I think much of the time that frustration comes from organizational disorientation. When that happens to pilots, the advice is to keep your eye on the horizon. For groups moving through time, developing a shared sense of destiny is the way to focus on the horizon, to get a fix on the North Star.

The prophet Daniel interpreted handwriting on King Belshazzar's wall (Daniel 5). For me, the "writing on the wall" was the mission statement of Taco Bell, Inc., which was hanging in the lavatory next to the sign reminding employees to wash their hands. (They could ponder their corporate mission while they scrubbed.) I can't remember what the sign said, but what struck me was the use of the word *mission* and the fact that everyone in the corporation was expected to know it. I was trying to identify what had been lost in so many churches and in the denomination I serve, and when I saw that sign I realized it was a sense of mission. I'm talking about the absence of a corporate spirit that those of us who constitute the church—congregations, pastors, laity, and the seminary—are actually involved in this grand and holy project in history. I'm talking about the pure and urgent sense of divine call captured in the movie "Blues Brothers," when Jake and Elwood stand in their black suits, white socks, and porkpie hats and announce with deadly seriousness, "We're on a mission from God."

Mission is a shared sense of destiny that requires a leadership that is systemic in nature. Jim Kouzes and Barry Posner describe it as a teaching process. "Teaching a vision—and confirming that the vision is shared—is a process of engaging constituents in conversations about their lives, about their hopes and dreams."[5] Christian leaders know all about that. They called Jesus "Rabbi," which is Hebrew for "teacher." They called themselves "disciples," which is Greek for "pupils." When Jesus gave the great commission, he said, "make disciples (students) of all nations" (Matthew 28:19, NRSV).

LISTEN DEEPLY

Part of the art of leadership is putting shared vision into words. The test of a vision is, finally, "Does the vision ring true?" As Lovett Weems reminds us, "Our best leaders tell us what we are thinking; our best leaders tell us what we are feeling."[6] When Irving Berlin died, Charles Kuralt said, "He eavesdropped on the American heart. When we heard his songs, we knew, 'That's us.'"[7] In turn, the Christian leader is lifted and challenged by the congregation. In the words of Leon Russell, "Your image of me is what I hope to be."[8]

And so, we listen deeply to others. Like a carpenter working with a fine piece of wood, there is a grain to every group, and an effective leader reads the grain.

In the African American church community, there is a tradition of "call and response." During the sermon, the congregation "talks back," affirming, encouraging, or withholding affirmation by their spontaneous spoken response to the message. The preacher is in a symbiotic relationship with the priesthood of all believers, even in the middle of the sermon.

We do this because we believe everyone has value as a child of God and because we believe everyone has a role to play in the Kingdom. We use the word *minister* sometimes to refer to the ordained clergy, but we believe that all baptized Christians are being called to some form of ministry. The churches I know that are growing and becoming more deeply engaged in mission are those that help their members discover their call and cultivate their spiritual gifts.

Betty Beene, one of the nation's leading experts on philanthropy, came to the presidency of the United Way of America in 1997, at a time when the United Way brand had been severely damaged by scandal (see Chapter Two). With morale collapsed and funds drying up, I'm sure Betty often used her favorite prayer, the Jesus Prayer: "Lord, have mercy on me. Make haste to help me."

Betty spent her first year crisscrossing the country to meet with local United Way volunteers and staff. In cities large and small, in urban, suburban, and rural settings, she heard firsthand the extent of the damage to the organization. It was clear that the institution's national standards for local United Way operations were critical to ensuring the consistent enactment of sound management practices and the restoration of the credibility of the United Way brand.

The temptation was there to draft a set of standards and deliver them like a pair of stone tablets to the chapters, in a decisive leadership style. Instead, Betty convened representatives of local staffs, boards of directors, donors, and leaders of agencies funded by the United Way from around the country. It was their task to develop the corporate (national) Standards of Excellence for local United Way operations. Meeting these standards would be required in order to use the United Way name and logo, as well as receive the benefits of national service, like joint promotions with the National Football League.

This participatory decision-making process took longer but generated confidence in the outcome by the majority of local United Ways, despite significant political opposition. Both the decision-making process and the end product redirected anger about the misdeeds of a few and transformed apathy about the future into energy. Betty applied the same approach to leadership she had always found true in fundraising. As she tells me often: "People support what they help to create."

SACRIFICE IS THE SOUL OF LEADERSHIP

A few years ago, on the Sunday after Hurricane Andrew struck Florida, the subject of relief efforts came up during the children's sermon. All of a sudden, five-year-old Loren Davis started talking. Loren was the shiest girl in the church, and everybody knew it. But this time, she spoke up. She had been thinking about the hurricane that left many children without a home. And then she said, "I have been given so much money and so many toys, I want to give those children my money and my toys." Of course, she was talking about a combined value of fifty dollars or so. But later, when the regular offering was taken up, there were all sorts of envelopes and checks with "hurricane" written on them. Fifty dollars produced $5,000, and the rest of the offering was nearly a record day in the history of that church.[9]

Loren's equation, "I have been given so much. . . . I want to give," is the fundamental dynamic of Christianity. We experience all the gifts from God, which we call "Grace," and especially the gift of Christ. And our response is gratitude—a source of new life and new possibilities.

What does this have to do with leadership? The central theme of the Christian faith is sacrifice, which is the redemptive power. It is what makes our history more than nostalgia and makes our teachings more than philosophical speculation. It is what the Cross is all about. Christians of all times and places gather around the sacrificial table to share in the body and the blood. It is how we become the Body of Christ in the world. This is what separates us from the world: we proclaim Christ crucified.

St. Paul says this message of the Cross is "foolishness" to everyone else (1 Corinthians 1:23, NRSV). And yet that foolishness is rooted in a fundamental fact of human existence and is a deep lesson for all leaders: sacrifice is at the soul of leadership. Jesus himself spoke of this: "This is my commandment, that you love one another as I have loved you. No one has greater love than this, to lay down one's life for one's friends" (John 15:12–13, NRSV). Great leadership we have known, in battle or in peace, is sacrificial in nature. It is as if the height of the vision must be proportional to the depth of the sacrifice. It is the fundamental act of believing in the future.

Shortly before she was assassinated, Indian Prime Minister Indira Gandhi was asked what she and other Hindu figures (like Mahatma Gandhi) thought was the main contribution of the faith tradition of Mother Theresa. Gandhi thought it is our concept of a God who sacrifices himself. "People are dying to give their lives away," she said.[10]

People sense that the great question in life is not between life and death. We are all going to die. The question is: What are you living for? Or what are you dying for? It is the same question.

GIVE LIFE TO YOUR VISION

Leaders teach vision constantly, sometimes with words and sometimes through rich nonverbal and symbolic forms of communication.

Christians were learning long before they could read or even understand the Latin of the mass. We are taught through the rituals of the church, especially baptism and holy communion. We are taught by the symbols: the cross, the sign of the fish, the shields of the apostles, the shroud on Good Friday, the flowers at Easter. In differing practices from various denomination, we learn through all the senses: the sight of a flame, the sound of the bells, the taste of communion wine, the smell of incense, and the feel of the prayer bead.

When we use words, it is most often in story so that all of us might find our personal stories in the larger story. We tell the stories of the Old Testament, which are the epic stories of destiny. And we tell the stories that Jesus told—the parables. The parables are all essentially the same; they are all designed to teach about the Kingdom, many beginning: "The Kingdom of God is like. . . . " They are structured like a joke (picture Jesus smiling as he tells them), always containing that surprise change in perspective as the world as it is today is compared with the way it can be.

Humans are creatures of habit, so much of Christian leadership should provide opportunities to form habits of the mind and heart. Our visions come to life through spiritual disciplines like prayer, fasting, devotional reading, and service. These disciplines usually involve memorization, which forms the infrastructure for the visionary mind. Children learn to recite the Lord's Prayer, the Apostles' Creed, and the 23rd Psalm long before they know what they mean and before they *need* to know.

And we teach by our actions. People hold their leaders to a higher moral standing. And they should. As Christians, we have to literally "practice what we preach." Jesus taught the Kingdom vision when he washed the feet of the disciples. The Pope taught it when he visited his would-be assassin—and kissed him.

Leaders give life to a vision by making it tangible through a process of reverse engineering. Leaders ask, "What would success look like?" and "How can we organize to achieve these results?" Christians also ask, "What would success look like to God?" Most of the time, when a church goes through a round of strategic planning, someone ends up in the gospel of Matthew and finds the nineteenth verse of the twenty-eighth chapter: "go make disciples." And we look to the twenty-fifth chapter to find out what discipleship in the Kingdom looks like.

The disciples asked Jesus about results. They asked, "What will the signs be?" And he began again to teach about the Kingdom. And he told a story of those who would be judged successful. "Come and inherit the Kingdom, for I was hungry, and thirsty; I was a stranger, I was naked and I was in prison and you did something about it. They asked, when did we do this, and Christ answered, when you did this to the least of these my children, you did it to me."

Leadership is the ability to move people, to change their minds and hearts and actions. The Greek word for that kind of change is *Metanoia;* you find it translated in the Bible as "repent," as in, "Repent, for the Kingdom of Heaven is at hand" (Matthew 3:2, NKJV). Christians believe that kind of transformation is a gift from God. It isn't just a one-time, all-or-nothing change; it is synonymous with life itself, the turning from death to life. God works this transformation through the Holy Spirit. For us, it is the animating force, the change agent of human existence. And it is as close to us as our next breath, for *Spirit* is a word for *breath*. Others borrow this concept when they use that word with a small "s" as in the phrase *team spirit* or in the words *inspiration* and *aspiration.*

Christian leadership is more like being on a sailboat than a rowboat. Christian leaders are not the source of Spirit; they are more like respiratory therapists. They are ushers, servants, midwives, spokespersons, and witnesses to the presence of the Holy Spirit at work in the world.

Leadership that is spiritual (with a small "s") takes seriously that there is a force at work in every organization. The energy for change is not a function of how hard the leader pushes. There is something else at work that transcends the time-management chart and the performance indicators. It's the difference between the job and the vocation—the calling.

Questions for Reflection

1. When have my organization and I struggled and survived? What is the story of my struggle? What are the teachable lessons from this story?
2. What time of day and where am I most free from the tyranny of the present? Could I use that time for prayer and Bible study, especially those passages that speak of God's promise for the future? What could I do that would be a great adventure? What is the future state of affairs I desire and aspire to for my organization or neighborhood or family? What is pulling me forward?
3. What good news from my organization would get other members of my team on the front page of the newspaper? What would amazing success look like? What could I do that would help make us all proud to have worked here?
4. What images breathe life into my vision? How can I animate my vision and share it with others, using stories of hope and transformation?
5. When is the last time I prayed for those I lead? How well do I understand the stories, hopes, and aspirations of those around me? How can I create a future that weaves together our common aspirations?

PART THREE

Challenge the Process

The work of leaders is change. To them the status quo is unacceptable. Leaders *search for opportunities* by seeking innovative ways to change, grow, and improve. They seize the initiative to make things happen. And knowing they have no monopoly on good ideas, leaders constantly scan the outside environment for creative ways to do new things.

You can't get from here to tomorrow in one giant leap. Extraordinary things get done one step at a time. Leaders *experiment and take risks* by constantly generating small wins and by learning from mistakes. And, despite persistent opposition and inevitable setbacks, leaders demonstrate the courage to continue the quest.

5 REFLECTIONS ON CHALLENGE THE PROCESS

Patrick Lencioni

The greatest among you will be your servant. For whoever exalts himself will be humbled, and whoever humbles himself will be exalted.

Matthew 23:11–12, NIV

Should you then seek great things for yourself?

Jeremiah 45:5, NIV

If you were searching for leaders to change the world for the better, what qualities would you look for? Courage and intelligence would certainly be prime candidates. Charisma might make the list. Or even creativity.

As important—even essential—as these characteristics may be, I would have to rank two others ahead of them, especially when I think about a Christian leader. In fact, in my work with leaders, I have found many courageous, intelligent, charismatic, and creative people. But few of them possessed the two qualities that I'm thinking of: humility and pain tolerance. Let me explain what I mean.

When I graduated from college, like so many other eager young people I wanted to change the world. Call it what you will, I was determined to make a difference, defy conventional wisdom, confront the status quo, and challenge the process. At the time, I was sure that these lofty aspirations were noble. I was wrong. There were two big problems with my postgraduate zeal.

First, I had no specific idea about what kind of a difference I wanted to make. And although that may not seem like a big deal, it masked a larger one: I was more interested in being *recognized* for having changed the world than anything else.

Had I been pumped full of truth serum and pressed to choose one particular field in which I wanted to change the world, I probably would have said, "It doesn't really matter, as long as it is something unique, and I get credit for it." You see, making a difference was not really about the world after all. It was about me.

There was another problem with my desire to change the world, and it is just as important. Under the influence of a second dose of truth serum, I would have admitted that there were limits to my desire to change the world. As much as I wanted to make a difference, I wasn't too keen on having to suffer much along the way. "Sure, I can deal with some hard work. Maybe even temporary financial setbacks. But real suffering? Embarrassment? Rejection by loved ones? No thank you. I don't want to make *that* big a difference."

Before setting out on a quest to challenge the process and change the world, Christian leaders should probably ask themselves two questions: "Who am I really serving?" and "Am I ready to suffer?" Had I asked myself these questions right after college, I would have realized that I was in no position to challenge any process.

QUESTION 1: WHO AM I REALLY SERVING?

Ironically, most people see leaders who change the world as needing to be brazen and audacious. But the only way to make a real difference is to do so humbly, without regard for recognition, ego, pride, even self-preservation. Of course, Christ is our ultimate example of this kind of humility.

First, his mission was never about serving himself. In fact, he claimed no credit for what he said and did. "The words I say to you are not just my own. Rather, it is the Father, living in me, who is doing his work" (John 14:10, NIV).

Jesus sought no earthly glory for his miraculous deeds, often instructing those he cured not to tell others about him. Nor did he preach and live among a wealthy and celebrated set but rather with the poor, sick, and rejected. I think Christ would have answered the question "Who am I serving?" with two unequivocal answers: "My Father and His people."

A powerful example of humble, selfless leadership occurred in my life recently; it came from an unlikely source. For the past few years, I have been privileged to serve on the board of directors of the Make-A-Wish Foundation of America, an extraordinary organization that grants the wishes of children with life-threatening medical conditions to enrich the human experience with hope, strength, and joy. My spot on the board was created by Kevin Wartman, a quiet Christian man who had yet to complete his full six-year term.

Unlike me, a relative newcomer to the foundation, Kevin had dedicated years of his life and his personal time to the foundation, from volunteering as a wish granter to serving on the local Make-A-Wish board in Idaho.

Even though Kevin had been successful in his career, he was not the kind of guy who was being asked by CEOs to sit on prestigious corporate boards. Becoming a member of the national board of a well-known foundation was both an honor and a privilege for him, after years of selfless, hard work. Without a doubt, it provided Kevin with a sense of satisfaction and honor in his local chapter and community.

As the foundation grew in scope and awareness, the board (including Kevin) decided collectively that it should change the composition of its board to more closely resemble a higher-profile, more corporate model. Because of my work with CEOs and their companies, I became a candidate. But there was not an open spot on the board for me, so Kevin took it upon himself to step down.

He didn't do this because he wanted to spend more time with his family and less time with the foundation (I know this because he continues to volunteer his time and energy). And it wasn't because he had stopped enjoying being on the board. Kevin loved working with his colleagues. There was no escaping the fact that there was only one reason Kevin sacrificed something so valuable and personally meaningful—something he had earned over many years: he believed it was in the best interests of the organization and, ultimately, the children the foundation serves.

I have worked with many well-known and charismatic leaders in my career, but none have had a more profound impact on me as a leader than Kevin. Without saying a word, he demonstrated the power of putting the needs of others first and serving the greater good.

For a Christian leader, this subjugation of self to mission is paramount, because the only reason to challenge a process is to serve Christ. When we make ourselves more important than what we are trying to do, we diminish the focus on our mission and, ultimately, on Christ.

Politics always seems to be a good place to look for leaders who struggle with humility. I recently saw a few minutes of C-Span, a non-profit television station that broadcasts congressional votes, hearings, and other civic-minded events. I was watching a legislator who has been in Congress for many, many years, as he was conducting a hearing and lecturing one of the citizens who had been called to testify before a committee.

Now, the sound had been muted on the television, so I could not hear what was being said. But I remember how animated and full of conviction this congressman seemed to be. And then I recalled that every time I had seen him on TV, which was often, he always seemed just as animated and convicted as he was on that day. In fact, he always seemed to be flabbergasted at the people who appeared before him, and so he lectured and condescended to them, similar to the way a parent scolds ornery children.

I had never been terribly fond of this guy, who seemed determined to establish himself as a champion of change and the enemy of the status quo. And that's when I realized that if a person feels the need to challenge every process, to be constantly defying the status quo, there is a good chance that he is doing so because he wants to be known for that. Every issue cannot possibly warrant the same level of outrage and passion. One of my favorite sayings is this: "If everything is important, then nothing is." If we are looking too hard for issues to challenge, it is possible that we are in love with the process of challenging more than we are truly challenging a process. Jim Kouzes and Barry Posner are very clear about this problem: "Leadership is not about challenge for challenge's sake."[1] It is about the process being challenged, not the challenger of the process.

Which brings to mind another congressman, who has also been legislating for many, many years. He too is on television from time to time, but he never seems to be agitated or upset. He is more than happy to be a quiet expert and to let others take the lead and garner the attention.

Now, I like this senator's style more than the flamboyant one, for sure. But I am slightly troubled by his unwavering restraint. During his career, he has held a number of controversial and unpopular opinions based on his thorough knowledge and research on critical issues affecting national security, and in those cases he has usually been proved right in the end. And yet, he never seems to get upset with his colleagues when they fail to rally around his thinking. As a result, his impact on Congress and the nation is not nearly what it should be, given his experience, knowledge, and intelligence.

And so, I wonder whether he may be too determined to be liked universally, and that is what keeps him from standing up and shouting louder—which leads me to the second question for Christian leaders.

QUESTION 2: AM I PREPARED TO SUFFER?

When it came to paying the price for changing the world, Christ paid it in full. He not only accepted death on the cross but also real human pain, suffering, rejection, and ridicule along the way. Sometimes I think it is easy to overlook what this meant.

During a Good Friday ceremony a few years ago, a woman read an account by a doctor of how Christ died, that is, the specific physical torment that he would have endured, based on the kind of death he experienced. Crowned with thorns. Whipped. Spit upon. Forced to carry a heavy cross. Hands and feet punctured and fastened to wood. Pierced with a lance. His lungs filled with fluid. Unimaginable, excruciating pain.

Even beyond the unimaginable physical pain, Christ endured what we would consider to be incomprehensible ridicule and public humiliation. Here was the most holy man to walk the face of the earth, stripped of his clothes in public, spit upon, mocked by soldiers in front of his family, and even taunted by the criminals who were crucified next to him. Think about the reality of this scene.

It was by enduring the most brutal form of human suffering that Christ changed the world. Although few, if any of us, could even contemplate something like his pain, are we prepared to endure even something considerably less?

When I was a boy, I loved to read and learn about the Christians throughout history who had stood up against great forces and prevailed. There were saints such as John the Baptist, Peter, Paul, Joan of Arc, and St. Thomas Moore. In American history, there were other Christians, such as Abraham Lincoln and Martin Luther King Jr., who fit this mold in some ways. I had always seen these people as having led brave but glorious lives—the kind that would certainly merit praise and recognition from generations to come.

But then I got older and came to realize that each of these people shared a few tragic fates we often gloss over in history books. First and most obviously, they were all killed for their causes. Perhaps more important though is that they were all hated at times, not just by their enemies but by the very people they were trying to serve. And certainly, their own supporters grew tired of the uncompromising demands that they placed on themselves and others.

Still, I always imagined that they endured these difficulties by saying to themselves, "Oh, this is no big deal. After all, one day I'll be famous and admired for what I'm doing. It will all be worth it. And besides, the people I really care about are still supporting me."

But the fact is, many of these people died before they knew that their causes would ultimately prevail. They had no guarantees that they would be redeemed here on earth in the minds and hearts of even their loved ones. For that matter, many great leaders never became famous; they died lonely and defeated, their impact occurring long after their death—and maybe even then with no credit ever given to them. Did they fail? Of course not. But how were they measured by worldly standards?

PERSEVERE IN THE FACE OF CHALLENGE

Fortunately, it is unlikely that the people reading this book will ever have to endure torture or death in pursuit of challenging a process. (It is worth remembering that there are many around the world who cannot say this. They need our prayers and support.) But even for us who are blessed to work in a relatively peaceful organizational environment, the challenge of suffering is still very real. We can be fired by a manager, embarrassed in front of subordinates, or ridiculed by peers, all with traumatic impact on our self-esteem.

How do we prepare ourselves for this possibility? Jim and Barry talk about the importance of psychological hardiness. "People with a hardy attitude take change, risk, turmoil, and the strains of life in stride. When they encounter a stressful event—whether positive or negative—they react predictably. They consider the event engaging, they feel that they can influence the outcome, and they see it as an opportunity for development."[2]

But how do leaders become hardy when they face the possibility of real suffering? For a Christian leader, it comes from knowing that we are ultimately working for salvation and not short-term personal gain. Christ called his disciples to be hardy when he asked them, "Who of you by worrying can add a single hour to his life?" (Luke 12:25, NIV). And he sent them out to change the world and to face certain suffering by saying, "Do not worry about how you will defend yourselves or what you will say, for the Holy Spirit will teach you at that time what you should say" (Luke 12:11–12, NIV).

St. Paul of the Cross asked worshipers to be hardy when he said, "Take everything that happens as coming from the hands of God, who loves you; in this way every trial will become a source of peace and joy since God is not a burden, but rather comfort, joy and cheerfulness." As hard and even naïve as this may sound, it is what Christ calls us to do. Though we alone cannot hope to be so hardy, "with God all things are possible" (Matthew 19:26, NIV).

Beyond Humility and Suffering

For those rare leaders who are truly motivated by serving the greater good and who are willing to suffer in doing so, there are certainly many other concepts that allow them to achieve the greatest possible impact. The first has to do with enlisting others in the challenge at hand. Before exploring the best way to do this, it is worth looking at how to ensure that the right people are being enlisted.

In his book *Good to Great,* Jim Collins talks about the importance of "getting the right people on the bus."[3] He goes so far as to say that this may be the most important criterion in transforming an organization. Certainly, the same can be said for a leader who is assembling a team of individuals to make a difference in the world. The problem, of course, is how to decide whether someone belongs, and if they don't belong, how to make a change.

I have found that leaders make two basic mistakes when trying to get the right people on the bus. First, they want to avoid losing team members. But maintaining the status quo of a team cannot be more important than the desired outcome. Besides, change is often needed. Jim and Barry describe this aspect of team development by stating that, "Teams go through life cycles, just as products do. Even the best teams get stale and need to be refreshed."[4] Coming to terms with this is critical.

The second mistake I often see is that leaders who are okay with the possibility of changing the makeup of a team, erroneously assume the people they are evaluating are either "right" or "wrong." In other words, they put far too much energy into assessing people's aptitudes and not enough into enlisting them.

Making challenge meaningful to everyone means giving them a chance to find a connection to the challenge. A leader who is uncertain, even doubtful, about whether a team member is appropriately motivated would be well advised to take the most naked, obvious approach: come right out and say so. There is nothing wrong with saying, "I am deeply passionate about the challenge our team is taking on, and I want everyone on the team to share that passion. Not that it has to look and feel the same for you as it does for me, because we're all different. But commitment has to be there. And if, after we talk about this and completely understand it, you don't think that this is interesting or personally motivating, that's okay. Let's just be clear about it and find another organization or issue that fires you up."

If, after hearing this message, they decide to enlist in the challenge, terrific. If they decide they can't commit with the level of passion and energy you need, they'll often opt out without the bitterness and resentment that accompanies most separations. In those cases of separation when bitterness and resentment are unavoidable, you'll know you've given the person an honest chance to find a way to get on the bus. Remember, if you're really motivated by the challenge of serving others, then you owe it to yourself, your team, and the people you're serving to make sure everyone on the bus is committed.

Risk

Once the bus is full, what next? First, make sure the outcome is clear to everyone, and then let everybody drive. That's right. Everybody. Christ didn't say to his disciples at Pentecost, "Okay, who wants to speak in tongues? Can I have a show of hands? Who's interested in travel? Anyone?" He ensured that he had the right people on the bus, and then he gave each one of them a set of keys.

But what about those people who insist they don't want to drive? You need to help them take that risk. There will be others who won't be good drivers, and you know that. But *you'll* need to take the risk and let them drive anyway. Risk and error play a role in challenging the process. According to Jim and Barry, "It is absolutely essential to take risks. Over and over again, people in our study tell us how important mistakes and failure have been to their success. Without those experiences, they would have been unable to achieve their aspirations."[5]

And when failure occurs, because it will always occur, you will be faced with what Jim and Barry call a *moment of truth.* "The way that leaders handle crises says more about what they stand for than how they deal with stable, easy situations." Use that occasion to demonstrate your commitment to working through it for the common goal. Your team will not soon forget. (For more on handling crises, see *The Leadership Challenge,* pages 86–88.) And when it is a mistake that you, the leader, have made, the moment of truth is particularly powerful.

> We believe that leaders should apologize for and atone for their mistakes. After all, their mistakes may cause inconvenience, loss and possible injury. . . . Our evidence suggests that acting in ways to hide mistakes will be much more damaging and will, in fact, erode credibility. . . . By admitting you were wrong, you can build credibility rather than destroy it.[6]

And you can send a powerful message to your team about how to handle themselves in a similar circumstance.

Finally, being open to mistakes is not the same as allowing yourself to commit them haphazardly. Jim and Barry encourage leaders not to "attempt to accomplish too much at once, especially in the beginning. Break large groups and goals into small cohesive teams and doable tasks."[7] And don't underestimate the importance of incremental improvement. A marathoner can tell you that the ability to run 26.2 miles does not just happen in one day—it's a process. A runner must first start with short runs and then carefully add distance over time to work up to completing a marathon. The same principle applies to teams facing a challenge. "Make sure to include a few early successes in your plan. There's nothing more discouraging than being confronted initially with tasks that you don't know how to do and at which you know you'll fail."[8] A momentum of success is a force that even detractors cannot break.

Finding leaders who can challenge the process and change the world for the better is not easy. The truth is, it is rare to find a human being who can accept the requirements of true Christian leadership, setting aside ego and fear of suffering, failure, and rejection, which isn't such a surprise when one considers the nature of our humanity and our inclination toward sin and self-preservation. As it turns out, the world is not as difficult to change as its leaders are.

Questions for Reflection

1. How can I make sure that when I challenge the process and change the world, I do it for the sake of God and others? How can I make sure that it's not about me wanting to be recognized for being a challenger?

2. Where will I find and how will I maintain the strength and the courage to endure the inevitable mistakes and setbacks—and accompanying discomfort—that will occur? How can I learn from my mistakes and temporary failures?

3. I know there's not necessarily a straight path to the future. How can I break down the path into small steps, so each one moves us forward and increases momentum?

4. How can I find, develop, and enlist the help of people who share my commitment and lovingly leave behind those who do not? How can I help others reach beyond what they're doing today and try something new?

5. How can I create a climate in which people are willing to accept the mistakes that are unavoidable and necessary in breakthrough learning?

PART FOUR

Enable Others to Act

Leaders know they can't do it alone. It takes partners to get extraordinary things done in organizations. So, leaders *foster collaboration* by promoting cooperative goals and building trust. They develop teams with spirit and cohesion. They promote a sense of reciprocity and a feeling of "we're all in this together."

Leaders understand that mutual respect is what sustains extraordinary efforts. Leaders *strengthen others* by sharing power and providing choice, making each person feel competent and confident. They nurture self-esteem and sustain human dignity.

6 REFLECTIONS ON ENABLE OTHERS TO ACT

Nancy Ortberg

The work is too heavy for you, you cannot handle it alone . . .

select capable people . . . have them serve. . . . That will make

your load lighter, because they will share it with you.

Exodus 18:18, 21–22, NIV

Let us think about each other and help each other to show

love and do good deeds.

Hebrews 10:24, NCV

At Willow Creek Community Church, I direct a ministry called Axis, the weekend service that targets the eighteen-to-twentysomething generation. Every summer, we do a series called Axis at the Movies, in which we pick four Hollywood blockbusters, show them at our meetings, and then teach based on the movie themes.

August is always a hard month to plan for; everybody's out of town. So we thought, "What if we get a multidisciplinary team from Axis together to start brainstorming for the August dates?" We pulled together people from operations, administration, the creative team, and our small group leadership team. If you've ever had a leader and an artist in the same room together, you know you have your work cut out for you already. Somehow we got everybody on the same page to paint the vision and let the ideas flow.

As a result of the team effort, we put together a five-week series called 21-C, which focused on how to live an authentic faith in the twenty-first century. We brainstormed a list of four outside speakers and held Week 5 open for something special. As it turned out, we had our highest attendance for the month of August, which is typically one of our lowest-attendance months. All of this happened because we collaborated on a project and the team took ownership.

The first week of the series featured a young man named Shane Claiborne, who had spent a year with Mother Teresa and now runs a ministry called The Simple Way in Philadelphia. He and a small group of people live in abandoned housing with the homeless. They go to court with them. They feed them. They build relationships with them. He told us that the gospels contain more passages about the church's response to the poor than about doctrine or theology.

At the end of the service, Shane said, "I have a challenge for you. I'm going into the inner city of Chicago tonight, and I'd like to ask any of you that are called to take your shoes and socks off right now. While we stand up to worship, I want you to go to the back of the room and dump them off. I guarantee you homeless people will get them tonight."

Seventeen hundred pairs of shoes were dumped in the back of our room while we worshiped God. It was one of the most amazing experiences of my life. You could hear Velcro straps come off of sandals and shoes all across the activity center.

On Sunday morning the same thing happened. A number of Axis people were running across the hot blacktop to their cars, and an older couple from the church, as they were leaving the parking lot in their car, saw the barefoot kids. Annoyed at the sight, the husband rolled down his window and yelled, "What's going on?" A girl came over and told him excitedly what had happened. The man's eyes filled with tears. "We're going home and getting our shoes, too," he said. We had one of the most remarkable five-week runs in the history of Axis, and one of the reasons was that we collaborated as a team.

Shane demonstrated to all of us at Willow Creek that a leader can't do it alone. He showed us on that day at Willow Creek that if we all pull together, each and every person can contribute to clothing the homeless. He showed us that each of us makes a difference. "Great dreams don't become significant realities through the actions of a single leader," say Jim Kouzes and Barry Posner. "Leadership is a team effort."[1] A leader has no choice but to enable others to act, for it is only when people feel trusted, feel part of something, and feel strong and capable that they can get extraordinary things done.

JESUS AS A SERVANT LEADER

Jesus embodies the ultimate example of someone who fostered collaboration and strengthened individuals. A lot of people talk about Jesus as if he were a soloist. They seem to forget that a large part of his ministry was in collaboration with others.

Remember what he did with the band of men who followed him? He built a sense of teamwork and loyalty among this disparate group of twelve individuals and through them turned the world upside down. Jesus has been called the greatest leader of all time because he demonstrated servant leadership and made his disciples into team players.

One of the very first instances of Jesus' leadership was when he called the twelve disciples. And by doing that, he showed us this principle: *If what I'm called to do is going to last, the first thing I have to do is start with people in whom I can duplicate it.* After just three years with his disciples, Jesus knew that when he left they would be well equipped to continue. In the business world they call this team building. Jim and Barry refer to it as fostering collaboration.

As those three short years of training wound to a close, one of the last things Jesus did was turn the keys of the church over to Peter. I wouldn't have picked Peter; he had made so many mistakes. Remember the passage where Jesus is giving his final instructions to Peter on the shores of the Sea of Galilee? His question isn't, "Okay, Peter, are you going to screw up again?" That's what I'd be asking. Instead, Jesus just says, "Here's the most important question and answer: Do you love me, Peter? If so, then feed my sheep." So while his first act of leadership was to call and train the twelve disciples, his last act of leadership was to give the power away before he left.

IN THE TRADITION OF THE PRIESTHOOD OF ALL BELIEVERS

Enabling people to act is not some new leadership fad. It's based firmly in the biblical concept of the priesthood of all believers. In the Old Testament, as God looked down at this amazing place He had created, we see that He focused on one small country, Israel, and from there zeroed in on one desert, just south of Israel in the Sinai Peninsula. He further narrowed His focus to one place called the tabernacle, and one room of the tabernacle, the holy of holies. "Here I will dwell among my people," God said. Out of the nation of Israel, He chose one tribe, the Levites, and one priest from the line of Aaron, the high priest, to go into that holy of holies. Then He chose one day a year—the Day of Atonement—when one man could go in one room to be in the presence of God.

The book of Hebrews says that when Jesus died on the cross, everything changed. At that moment, the veil that separated the holy of holies from the rest of the tabernacle—symbolizing our separation from God—was torn in two. That single, supernatural act opened the presence of God up from one place, one day, and one person to the era of anywhere, anytime, anyone. Now each of us has access to God through Jesus Christ. Likewise, each of us has a part to play in fulfilling God's purposes on earth. Since the resurrection, each of us is part of "the priesthood of all believers."

Think of the story in John 16. When Jesus tells his disciples about his death, they are understandably sad and confused. But then Jesus says the strangest thing to them: "It is best for you that I go away." At first glance, those words just seem to add insult to injury. However, Jesus goes on to explain that in his physical presence on the earth, he is limited. But when he goes, God will send His Holy Spirit, who will reside in every believer. That means that this priesthood—every faithful follower of Christ—is empowered to do the work of the Lord on earth.

THE NEED TO TRUST

Teamwork and collaboration can only happen when people trust each other. As leaders, we have no trouble trusting ourselves. We have to learn to put the same trust in other people that we put in ourselves and then release them to do the work. We have to trust that the same God who energizes our gifts energizes others. Trust is the foundational element of any good leader, and it has to be earned. You have to lay a foundation of trust before people can individually do their best.

Jim and Barry tell us that "trust is built when we make ourselves vulnerable to other people whose subsequent behavior we cannot control."[2] Trust is not about making yourself vulnerable to safe people. The kind of trust a leader needs to spread throughout an organization is a trust that says, "I carry my safety within my heart because I trust in God, and He is the only One who will never let me down." With such childlike trust in God, you know you're safe, regardless of the trustworthiness of those around you. That is the courage of a leader.

Max De Pree, who has written some of the finest leadership books on the market, has become an informal mentor of mine. He taught me what I like to call the "ministry of questions." Whenever a leader asks questions, he or she is laying a groundwork that says, "This is a collaborative team effort. I'm not coming at you with all the answers." Collaboration builds trust.

Jesus was open to influence. He made himself vulnerable to others and was transparent. Jesus also asked a lot of questions. Imagine God in human flesh asking questions of mere humans. Yet in doing so,

Jesus gave us a pattern for drawing out the best in those we lead and embedding in them something that will last. It takes a lot of courage to admit you're wrong, to admit mistakes, and to accept someone else's ideas over your own. But I honestly think that as a leader, if you're not apologizing on a regular basis you're probably not leading well.

I called Max De Pree one day. I was in a tizzy about something, and he let me ramble for a while; then he said, "You know, Nancy, leaders are only right 50 percent of the time." I remember thinking, *Oh my gosh! I can do 50 percent!* I was trying to be right all the time, or 90 percent of the time, and it was wearing me out. Allowing your people to see your human side—hearing you say, "I'm sorry" or "I was wrong"—will take you off the pedestal (on which you can be admired but never emulated) and put you down on the ground with them, where they will say, "If she can do it, I can do it" or "If he can make it work, I can, too." That's the power of leadership, but it only comes when you fill an organization with trust.

You will never be able to develop teams to their full potential unless you create an environment of trust *person by person* in your organization. Trust allows for self-disclosure and mistakes, and good leaders don't wait for somebody else to initiate these conversations. Be the first on your team to say, "Here's where I have fallen short." You have no idea what these words will do to those who follow you.

GIVE YOUR POWER AWAY

Any organization is only as strong as its leadership and the people who follow that lead. So the obvious next question a leader must ask is, "How do I strengthen those I lead?" The answer may surprise you. *A wise leader strengthens people by giving power away.* Leaders place constituents, not themselves, at the center. Leaders use their power in service of others, not in service of themselves.

Before I went into full-time ministry, I worked as a registered nurse in the emergency room of a busy hospital. One ER doc was such an incredible leader that when he was on your shift, you knew things were going to go smoothly. You thought, "Today I'm going to be part of a team, I'm going to learn something, and I'm going to be a better nurse for it."

Other doctors would tell us what to do, and we just did it. But this guy orchestrated the emergency room. He asked questions while he was calling for procedures. He wanted to know, "Why are we doing this?" He would say to his staff, "What do you think?" as he worked with a patient. He never lost control of the situation, but he conducted the team like a fine-tuned orchestra, because he involved everybody. Obviously, he stayed the leader; he made the calls. But it was not uncommon for him to ask someone for an opinion, obtain a vital piece of information, and then change his mind. By working under such a leader, I felt like I was part of saving lives, not just working a shift. He gave us critical tasks to do, and we rose to the challenge. He called us by our names and asked for feedback. And at the end of the shift, he always thanked everybody. Who wouldn't want to follow a leader like that?

Put Love into Action

Once a year in the Axis ministry I lead at Willow Creek Community Church in Chicago, we do a huge retreat. We shut down our weekend services for it and pull out all the stops. It is through this core-building retreat that we assimilate new people. It's my job and I get paid for doing it, so I normally lead this massive event. But last year, I sensed God telling me to hand the reins of this project to somebody else.

After I prayed about it, a volunteer named Bonnie came to mind. Bonnie was floored to be asked, but I knew she was immensely capable. I told our paid staff that for the next six months, Bonnie would be our leader. "I'm giving her reins to this entire retreat," I told the staff. I could see by their faces that they didn't quite believe me. They expected me to keep grabbing power back. But I let Bonnie call the meetings, lead the meetings, delegate the responsibilities, and follow up. She was amazing. We doubled the attendance of our retreat that year.

This was obviously a challenge to my ego because I had to deal with the fact that Bonnie did a better job than I did. I had to sit in meetings with my staff and watch Bonnie put calendars up on the wall and systematize the entire process, and I imagined everyone thinking, *Nancy couldn't do that.* They're right, I couldn't. I can create a vision for something, but you start getting details and dates and putting up little tiny boxes and I'm out of the room. So I made myself sit there and watch my staff learn to experience work under the leadership of a volunteer.

People thrive when they have meaningful work to do. Don't have people simply lick envelopes if they are capable of more. Don't give them mindless work because you couldn't think of anything else to do. Give them something critical to the advancement of your mission.

Another example is Willow Creek's cars ministry, which gave away twelve hundred free vehicles to single mothers last year alone. It started ten years ago with a guy named Bob, a member of the congregation who spotted a need and had an idea for how to solve it. Bob stood about six feet five and was covered in tattoos. After a sermon one Sunday, he came down to the front of the auditorium and waited in line to talk to our senior pastor, Bill Hybels.

"I've been going to this church for about six months, and it's changed my life," he told Bill. "I want to give back."

Bill took him seriously. "What do you think you want to do?"

"Well, I know what I can't do," Bob said. "I can't preach like you. The only thing I know how to do is be a mechanic. I drive on campus here and notice you have a lot of wealthy people that drive nice cars. I've also noticed something else. A lot of poor people go to this church too, and I see the types of cars they drive. A lot of them are single moms. So I was thinking, what if we do a clinic once a month and you let me use the pole barn in the back of the property? You advertise and have all the single moms bring their cars, and you ask all the people that drive those nice cars to give some money. We'll buy the parts and I'll do the labor and fix the cars."

What started as a simple idea that a leader took seriously evolved into a ministry that makes our church unique in its area. As a result,

Willow Creek is known as a place that takes care of the poor. That type of love in action affects people in ways talking never will.

Develop Talent Radar

Developing what I call talent radar is yet another way to give your power away. You don't just give away important tasks; you give them to the right people. As a leader, learn what areas of strength each person on your team possesses (you may have heard these referred to in the church as spiritual gifts). Everybody is good at something. Become a talent expert. Be on the lookout for clues by the way people respond to a situation. They're giving you information about what they're good at. For example, somebody who is gifted in administration will already have thoughts about breaking a problem down into manageable components. Do whatever it takes to get educated in spotting individual strengths in others: take classes, read books, attend seminars.

Michael Novak, a former U.S. ambassador and author of *Work as a Calling,* says, "One of the ways to spot what somebody is really good at is to look for the presence of enjoyment and a sense of renewed energies when they do something."[3] People who are operating in their spiritual gifted area are going to have renewed energies; they'll be invigorated by doing that task. When you give them a task that falls in their area of giftedness, they'll say things like, "I could do this forever."

As you give away power, be careful not to overlook people. Everyone has an area of giftedness—everyone. They may not know it, and sometimes the job of a leader is to see it for them before they can see it for themselves.

One of my favorite passages in the Bible is found in 1 Samuel, where the prophet Samuel is appointed to crown the new king of Israel before God breaks it to the old king that he's out of a job. Samuel is nervous, so God says, "All you have to do is go down there and anoint him, and then you can leave." Samuel agrees to go. So he journeys to the home of Jesse, and Jesse parades his sons in front of the prophet. Samuel is convinced the first son is God's chosen man.

By outward appearance, he's a natural leader—a big, strapping man. But a little voice inside Samuel's heart says, "Not this one." And that voice repeats itself with every son Jesse parades by until finally, in exasperation, Samuel says to Jesse, "Do you have any other sons?"

Jesse scratches his head and says in a dismissing way, "Well, there's David—the youngest—but he's out in the field with the sheep."

Samuel's reply is priceless: "I will not sit down until you bring him to me." History tells the rest of the story.

Fan People's Gifts into Flames

After you've given critical tasks to the right people, your commitment as a leader is to develop their character and their competence. This requires an investment of time and energy on your part, but like all the other aspects of *enabling people to act*, it pays high dividends.

During my first year of leading Axis, I met a charismatic guy named Jim. He's the kind of person you would give your right arm to have on your team. He influences people, and they flock to him. Jim was so anxious to get involved in Axis that he would corner me and tell me all the ideas he had for the ministry. I had an uneasy feeling about him, even though I liked him immensely. Somehow I sensed he was the type of guy who flitted from one thing to another, wherever the energy or new thing was.

"Tell you what let's do, Jim," I said. "Six months from now, let's see if you're still around and still interested. If you are, we'll talk." To this day I don't know why I said that. Call it intuition, a hunch. Jim told me later that it almost made him leave our ministry. He was angry with me. But a couple of days into the process, he realized what I was doing. I was waiting to see if he had character—if he was going to stick around—because I needed to develop leaders who were going to be in the ministry long term.

I watched Jim out of the corner of my eye for six months and never said anything more than a passing hello to him. I watched him hunker down and serve with quiet persistence, with no spotlight and no attention. He did the right things; he did them for the right reasons, and he did them for a long enough time that I thought, "I want that guy on my team." Now Jim has oversight of two critical areas in Axis that are flourishing under his leadership.

Character and competence are developed over time, and there's no way to microwave it. Your commitment as a leader is to say, "Over time, as you're overseeing this critical task, I will watch you and call character and competency issues into the conversation. At the same time, I will encourage you, and I promise you I will do everything to develop you. If I sense there's something in you that I can't develop, I will find other people who can and I will bring them into play in your life. I will make sure your gift is fanned into flame (see 2 Timothy 1:6) so it becomes strong and vibrant and serves others well."

Thirty years ago, Max De Pree was asked to serve on the board of trustees at Fuller Seminary. At the same time, the seminary asked a young leader named David Allen Hubbard to take over the presidency of the school. After David's inauguration, Max said, "David, I am committed to your success." Max humbled himself to be used by God for thirty years to develop character and competence in the person he perceived to be God's man for the leadership role. *I am committed to your success.* Those are some of the most powerful words a leader can say to the people he or she leads.

Make Heroes of People

The smallest leaders I know need all the attention for themselves. The leadership of one person is way too small to represent all that a thriving business or group or church should be. Make heroes of your people when they do things well. Put them up in front of people and tell their stories.

Two hero stories I share regularly come from the Axis group. Once a month, a team from Axis goes to visit kids in the Illinois Youth Correctional (IYC) facility. It is unglamorous and dirty—not a high-profile ministry. Claire, a woman from our congregation, wanted to be a part of the team on an ongoing basis. Over time, Claire started to build relationships with the girls at the IYC. Nothing remarkable, you might say. But what is remarkable to me about Claire's choice is that she is twenty-four years old and has been in a wheelchair since she was a toddler. She breathes through a ventilator and has significant physical limitations. Here's a young woman who has every reason to stay at home and be furious with God because she will probably never get married, never have children, and never walk, yet she chose instead to be a servant and minister to girls behind bars. I told Claire's story in Axis because I think she is a hero.

Evangelism is a huge part of Axis, and we are constantly trying to think of ways to motivate people to do personal evangelism in their lives. One of our guitar players, a guy named Sean, kept thinking of ways he could do this. It took him months to come up with the idea, but now every Thursday night Sean and a few people from Axis go to Champs (a sports bar) and do karaoke. They've formed relationships with the bartenders and waitresses and the people who hang out at the bar. Sometime later we had a "decision night" in Axis, and one bartender and two waitresses committed their lives to Christ because Sean went to the bar. Sean is a hero to me.

Find ways to make heroes of your people.

Lead Out of a Servant's Heart

The leader who tells everybody what to do and expects immediate obedience, without the motivation that comes from watching a servant leader at work, creates a workforce of implementers. This type of leader creates what has been called malicious compliance. You get the behavior you want on the outside, but nothing changes on the inside. Although this kind of action looks good on the surface, in reality, it breeds undesirable qualities like cynicism and lack of trust—subtly powerful forces that may not initially affect the outcome but eventually weaken the goal, the team, the organization. But when you lead out of a servant's heart, you tap into the best level of motivation in a person. Without the element of servant leadership, the farthest you will get into someone's motivation is the "have to" level. Over time, that will build a narrow, thin organization.

When a leader is able to drive down deeper and get to the "I want to" motivation, the organization becomes a type of perpetual motion machine. It no longer takes as much energy from you as a leader because you've built into those around you the zeal to do a job well. The "sustain" you've tapped in your team will carry all of you, collectively, well into the future. But remember, you can never develop other people as long as you hold on to the power. The power base has to be shared. It's no coincidence. Jesus did not talk about leadership very often, and every time he did, he talked about serving.

When Jesus served people, he called for them to turn their lives upside down. He was constantly going for the deeper motivations and the part in them that was created in the image of God—the part that says, "I can be more than this." He didn't just walk around getting coffee for people and patting them on the back. That's not what it means to serve. Serving means that when this person leaves my leadership sphere of influence, he or she will be a better person and leader because of the time spent with me.

As I think about which values of the Christian faith are most important to a godly leader, the list quickly narrows to four things: *integrity, authenticity, joy,* and *dignity of work.* If you as a leader can build an environment around those four values, you will create a place where people want to work.

The degree to which you are able to build trust and give your power away directly affects the kind of organization you grow. And ultimately, that trust comes down to what is between you and God. This is where it all starts and stops with a leader. If your trust in God can't be shaken, you will build trust no matter where you go. When all your leadership successes are memories and you draw your last breath, this is the only thing that will matter: the assurance that God is with you and that what you did counted.

May we learn to see people through God's eyes and enable them to act. May we learn to make heroes of those we lead. I'm grateful that many people modeled these leadership practices for me and for you. Someday, let it also be said of us that we came alongside and helped another human being flourish in their calling.

No matter where you serve as a leader, serve in such a way that when people leave your presence, they stand a little taller and smile a bit longer and say to themselves, "There's something different about that place."

Questions for Reflection

1. Who first enabled me to act? What is the primary leadership action I think of when this person comes to mind?
2. Have I created a "safe" environment for those under my leadership? How can I foster trust among the people I lead? In what ways can I bring people together so that they can see areas of commonality?
3. What makes me reluctant to share my power and influence with other people? What do I need to do to increase my comfort level with giving my power way?
4. Are there people on our team whose talents I've overlooked? How can I share more information with others? How would I increase the amount of discretion and choice that people have?
5. What specific actions come to mind when I hear the phrase *servant leader?*

PART FIVE

Encourage the Heart

The climb to the top is arduous and steep. People become exhausted, frustrated, and disenchanted. They're tempted to give up.

To keep hope and determination alive, *leaders need to recognize contributions* by showing appreciation for individual excellence. Genuine acts of caring uplift spirits and strengthen courage.

On every winning team, the members need to share in the rewards of their efforts. So *leaders should celebrate the values and the victories* by creating a spirit of community. That means expressing pride in the accomplishments of their team and making everyone feel like everyday heroes.

REFLECTIONS ON ENCOURAGE THE HEART

Ken Blanchard

My heart took delight in all my work, and this was the

reward for all my labor.

Ecclesiastes 2:10, NIV

Well done, thou good and faithful servant.

Matthew 25:21, NIV

Over the years, I think the most important concept I have ever taught is to accentuate the positive and catch people doing things right. That's what Encourage the Heart—the fifth and final practice of exemplary leadership—is all about.

When you talk about Encourage the Heart from a Christian perspective, it makes sense to focus our discussion on Jesus' leadership point of view:

Jesus called them together and said, "You know that the rulers of Gentiles lord it over them, and their high officials exercise authority over them. Not so with you. Instead, whoever wants to become great among you must be your servant, and whoever wants to be first must be your slave—just as the Son of Man did not come to be served, but to serve, and to give His life as a ransom for many." (Matthew 20:25–28, NIV)

In his "not so with you" instructions to his first disciples on how they were to lead, Jesus sent a clear message to all those who would follow him that leadership has to be first and foremost an act of service. No Plan B was implied or offered in his words. He placed no restrictions or limitations of time, place, or situation that would allow us to exempt ourselves from his command. For a follower of Jesus, servant leadership isn't just an option; it's a mandate.

I never thought of Jesus as a leadership role model until after *The One Minute Manager*[1] was published in 1982 and was a raving success. Suddenly, on becoming a best-selling author, I was either going to get a big head and think I was a big deal or wonder what was going on. I chose wonderment and, in the process, opened myself to the thought that it was "a God thing." Shortly afterwards, I was asked to appear on "The Hour of Power," televised from the Crystal Cathedral. While talking with me about the book, Dr. Robert Schuller suggested that Jesus was the classic One Minute Manager. After all, Jesus was very clear on goals, and the first secret of the One Minute Manager is One Minute Goal Setting. Then Jesus wandered from one village to another, always looking to see if he could catch someone doing something right. When people showed any sign of believing in him and the news he brought, Jesus would heal them, praise them, and encourage them. The second secret of the One Minute Manager is One Minute Praisings.

Finally, if people were off base, Jesus wasn't afraid to redirect them or chastise them. The final secret of the One Minute Manager is One Minute Reprimand.

Reverend Schuller's comments about Jesus as a One Minute Manager got me thinking. As I began to deepen in my faith and delve into the Bible, I quickly realized that everything I've ever taught or wrote about, Jesus did. And he did it perfectly with twelve inexperienced people. After studying leadership for over thirty years, I came to the conclusion that Jesus is the greatest leadership role model of all time. As a result of that insight, I cofounded the Center for FaithWalk Leadership, with the explicit purpose of challenging and equipping people to lead like Jesus.

As we explore what it means to lead like Jesus when it comes to encouraging the heart, I will examine two internal domains: the *heart* (motivation or intent) and the *head* (beliefs and leadership point of view). I will also examine two external domains: the *hands* (behavior and action) and the *habits* (discipline and commitment). We may be able to keep our motivations and beliefs (*heart* and *head*) inside, but our behavior and commitments (*hands* and *habits*) will affect others and determine how they follow.

THE HEART

Over the years, I got discouraged when I saw how many leaders had trouble with the concept of catching others doing things right. "Why aren't people following up?" I wondered. "Why aren't they getting it?" One day, I got a blinding flash of the obvious. I was starting in the wrong place. I was trying to change leaders from the outside in. I was beginning with behavior: what people do. I realized that what people do is always motivated by what's in their heart. Gradually, I realized that character and other fundamental heart qualities are critical indicators for determining behavior.

Theoretically, you could behave as though you were encouraging the heart, but if your intentions were not to help make people better at what they do, it would merely be manipulation. You would be encouraging them to gain something for your own sake.

Serve Others' Interests

Exemplary leaders serve others' interests, not their own. The crux of encouraging the heart lies in the answer to one key character question that is centered in your heart: Are you a servant leader or a self-serving leader? Few, if any, people would ever admit that they are self-serving leaders. And yet the reality is that many are. How do you tell the difference between a servant leader and a self-serving leader? Gordon MacDonald, in his classic book *Ordering your Private World*,[2] gave us a good hint when he identified two kinds of people in the world: *driven* people and *called* people.

Driven people think they own everything. They own their relationships. They own their possessions. They own their position. As a result, they spend most of their time protecting what they own. Everything they do is determined by their own self-interest. And so if they praise or encourage you, they're really doing it for their own good. Called people, on the other hand, think everything in life is on loan. Their relationships are on loan. Their possessions are on loan. Their position is on loan. As a result, they are not defensive or protective about their position as a leader. In fact, if a better leader comes along, they will partner with that person—sometimes even step aside and take a different role—because the only reason they are leading is to serve other people. If catching people doing things right helps others, they are eager to do it, not for their own benefit but for the benefit of those they lead. This character trait defines servant leadership. For the servant leader, the main reason for leading is to help other people win. Put another way, it's to help people *live according to the vision God placed inside them.*

The key to a servant leader's heart is humility. People with humility don't think less of themselves; they just think of themselves less. As Jim Collins suggests in his book *Good to Great*,[3] when things go well, leaders with humility look out the window and give everybody else the credit. They remain humble and unassuming about the success. When things go poorly, they look in the mirror and say, "What could I have done differently that would have helped these people be the best they could be?" Servant leaders take the hit. They know that all people are human and make mistakes.

In contrast, when things go well for self-serving leaders, they look in the mirror and beat on their chests like King Kong, thinking how great they are. But when things go wrong, they look out the window and blame everybody else. They're so self-absorbed, everything is filtered through an "I" orientation rather than a "we" orientation. People who work under this type of leader eventually get discouraged.

A helpful way to tell the difference between a servant and a self-serving leader is to watch how they react to feedback. Here's the test: If you offer leaders feedback about how they are leading and they "kill the messenger," they're self-serving. By giving them feedback, you have ignited their worst fears. You have pointed out a flaw in their leadership. They think that means you don't want them to lead anymore. And to lose their position, which defines who they are, is their worst nightmare. As a result, they have to dismiss you and your feedback. Self-serving leaders are only interested in maintaining their position and maintaining control.

If you give servant leaders feedback, however, they consider it a gift. Suppose you receive a wonderful gift for the holidays. What do you say to the gift giver? "Thanks! Where did you buy it? Are there any special instructions?" Similarly, if you give feedback to servant leaders about something they've done, they will say, "Thank you. How helpful. I didn't intend to do that. Is there anyone else I should talk to? Tell me more." Servant leaders love feedback because the only reason they're leading is to serve. If you can help them serve better, everybody wins.

If leaders are to be exemplary, they must encourage the heart. That begins with the heart question, "Am I a servant leader or a self-serving leader?" It is a question that, when answered with brutal honesty, will go to the core of your intent as a leader. Jesus was quick to answer this question. He did not come to be served but to serve.

The reality is that we're all self-serving to a degree because we come into this world with a self-serving heart. There is nothing more self-serving than a baby. A baby doesn't come home from the hospital asking about how he or she can help around the house. The journey of life is to move from a self-serving heart to a serving heart. You finally become an adult when you realize that life is about what you give rather than what you get. Now your focus is on encouraging the hearts of others.

Be Grounded in God

It is important to recognize that there is a flip side to encouraging the hearts of your people. Before we as leaders can encourage others, we have to have a source of encouragement for ourselves. But if you need a lot of external recognition, stop and take a look at your own self-esteem. I've heard it said that the devil's definition of self-worth is that *who you are is a function of your performance plus the opinion of others.* If the devil can hook you on that, he's got you, because now your focus is on fearing people, not fearing God. Once you get caught in that trap, you're just trying to keep up with the Joneses and look good.

Realize that God loves you unconditionally. Good parents love their children whether or not they are successful, so why should we expect less of God? Imagine what would happen inside our spirits if we accepted that unconditional love for ourselves? Make sure your self-worth is grounded in the knowledge of God's unconditional love for you, and remember that God doesn't make junk. When I, as a leader, start with "God confidence," I can be a servant leader to others because my heart is full of unconditional love.

THE HEAD

The journey of servant leadership that starts in the heart with motivation and intent must travel through another internal domain, that of the head, which is the leader's belief system and perspective on the role of leader.

All great leaders have a specific leadership point of view that defines how they see their role and their relationships to those they seek to influence. In particular, I want you to first understand the servant leadership point of view modeled and taught by Jesus and then learn what changes in thinking are required to align your own thinking about leadership with his as you think about encouraging the heart.

When I talk about servant leadership, most people think that means the inmates are running the prison. Servant leadership begins with a clear and compelling vision that excites the passion and the commitment of those who follow. In *Full Steam Ahead!*, which I coauthored with Jesse Stoner,[4] we contend that a good vision has three parts:

1. *Purpose/Mission: What business are you in?* When Walt Disney started his theme parks, he knew how to excite people. He said, "We are in the happiness business—we make magic." That clear purpose drives everything the cast members (employees) do with their guests (customers). Jesus had a clear mission with his disciples. He wanted them to become "fishers of men" (Matthew 4:19, NIV).

2. *Preferred Picture of the Future: What will your organization look like if everything is running as planned?* Walt Disney's picture of the future was expressed in the charge he gave every cast member: "Keep the same smile on people's faces when they leave the park as when they enter." He didn't care whether a guest was in the park two hours or ten hours. He just wanted to "keep them smiling."

Jesus outlined his picture of the future when he charged his followers to "go make disciples of all nations, baptizing them in the name of the Father and of the Son and of the Holy Spirit" (Matthew 28:19, NIV).

3. *Values: How do you want people to behave when they are working on your purpose and picture of the future?* Fewer than 10 percent of organizations around the world have clear, written values. But values are important because they drive people's behavior while they are working on the purpose and the picture of the future. Most organizations that do have values either have too many values or their values are not in rank order. Research shows that people can't focus on more than three or four values if you really want to have an impact on behavior. Also, values must be ranked to be effective. Why? Because life is about value conflicts. When these conflicts arise, people need to know which value they should focus on. Walt Disney intuitively knew this when he ranked safety ahead of other values: courtesy, the show, and efficiency. Why did he do that? Because he knew that if a guest left the park on a stretcher, that guest would not have the same smile on her face that was present when she entered

the park. So if a cast member heard a scream while being courteous to a guest, he would excuse himself immediately and focus on the number-one value—safety.

When the Pharisees asked Jesus what the greatest commandment was, his answer dealt with both the number of commandments and their rank order when he said, "Love the Lord your God with all your heart and with all your soul, and with all your mind. This is the first and greatest commandment. And the second is like it: Love your neighbor as yourself. All the law and the prophets hang on these two commandments" (Matthew 22:37–40).

Once you have a clear vision, goals can be set that help people focus their energy on a day-to-day basis. But now these goals take on bigger meaning, because they are in the context of a clear vision.

Have a Compelling Vision

In *The Leadership Challenge,* Jim Kouzes and Barry Posner talk about the importance of focusing on clear standards as a component of encouraging the heart. They compare the lack of standards—or what we would call a compelling vision—to a croquet match in *Alice in Wonderland:*

> Everyone kept moving and the rules kept changing all the time. Poor Alice. There was no way of knowing how to play the game to win. Besides, it was all rigged in favor of the Queen. We've all been Alice at one time or another in our lives. We've been at a place where we're not sure where we're supposed to be going, what the ground rules are that govern how we behave, or how we're doing along the way. And just when we get the hang of it, the organization comes along and changes everything. This is a recipe for maddening frustration and pitiful performance. Our hearts just aren't in it.[5]

Contrast that with an organization whose leadership communicates a clear and compelling vision and goals. Everybody wins. If leaders want people to give their all and put their hearts into the work, leaders must make sure people know where they are going. A compelling vision sets the stage for action. Goals release the energy to get the job done. They also provide the basis for catching people doing things right and for recognizing them for it. Rewards and recognition are much more meaningful when they are in support of a clear vision and goals.

The traditional hierarchy is good for the visionary aspect of leadership. People look to the leader for vision and direction, and although a leader should involve experienced people in shaping direction, the ultimate responsibility remains with the leader and cannot be delegated to others.

Live the Vision

However, the implementation role—living according to the vision and accomplishing the goals—is where most leaders and organizations get into trouble. The traditional hierarchy too often is kept alive and well, leaving the customers neglected at the bottom. All the energy in the organization moves up the hierarchy as workers try to please and be responsive to their bosses. This authoritarian structure too often forces the frontline customer-contact people to act like ducks and quack things like, "It's our policy," "I just work here," or "Do you want to talk to the supervisor?" In this environment, self-serving leaders assume "the sheep are there for the benefit of the shepherd." All the energy in the organization flows up the hierarchy.

Effective implementation requires turning the hierarchy upside-down so the customer-contact people are at the top of the organization, where they can soar like eagles in responding to customers, while leaders serve the needs of their people, helping them to live according to the vision and goals of the organization.

That's what Jesus had in mind when he washed the feet of the disciples. As he did that, Jesus was not implying they should go out and help people do anything they wanted. The vision and goals were clear. He got them from the top of the hierarchy—his Father. When it came to implementing the vision, he wanted them to be servant leaders and help people live according to the "good news."

THE HANDS

The journey to effective servant leadership turns outward when the heart and mind now guide the behavior (the hands) of the leader in interaction with those who follow. This is where good intention and right thinking start to bear good fruit. It is where real discipleship is truly tested.

In *The One Minute Manager,* Spencer Johnson and I wrote, "People who feel good about themselves produce good results."[6] That simple statement is so true. People who feel good about themselves work harder. The only problem, we discovered, is that if you focus too much on making others feel good, you can quickly get caught up in a human relations trap, focusing only on relationships. The reality is, you also need results. The real value behind encouraging others goes much deeper than that. Later, in *Putting the One Minute Manager to Work,* that quote was changed to read, "People who produce good results feel good about themselves."[7] By turning it around, I believe the emphasis got placed in the better order. Feeling good results from doing good work. Everything I do now as I instruct leaders is built around the question, How do we help people perform better? I do it because that's what makes people feel good about themselves and encourages their hearts.

The key to behaving like a servant leader is to become a performance coach and consider people's development to be just as important as their performance. There are three parts of performance coaching: *performance planning,* where you set goals and objectives; *day-to-day coaching,* where you help people win or accomplish their goals, and *performance evaluation,* where you evaluate people's performance over time.

Self-serving leaders spend most of their time on evaluation. They want to protect the hierarchy by sorting people out into performance categories. Servant leaders, however, focus on performance planning and day-to-day coaching. First, they want their people to be clear on what is expected of them and what good performance looks like.

Then they turn the traditional hierarchy upside-down and focus their energy on day-to-day coaching and helping people win. This is where Jesus spent most of his time. When he called his disciples to follow him, Jesus pledged to them his full support and guidance as they developed into "fishers of men." This is the duty of a servant leader— the ongoing investment of the leader's life into the lives of those who follow. Through their hands (effective leader behavior), they are able to transmit what is in their heart and head about servant leadership.

It is in the day-to-day coaching aspect of people development that we really encourage the heart. In doing that, there are certain things that we have to remember.

Pay Attention

Being mobile goes with the territory of being a leader, Jim and Barry assert. I have to agree. In fact, they note that at its root the word *lead* comes from an Old English word that means "go, travel, guide." Tom Peters and Bob Waterman didn't invent "management by wandering around." Jesus did. He wandered from one little town to another little town. If he caught people doing something right, he was willing to praise and to heal them. If they got off base, he was willing to redirect them and get them back on course.

As Jim and Barry observe in *The Leadership Challenge,*

> [Management by wandering around is not] purposeless wandering. Leaders are out there for a reason. One of the reasons . . . is to show that you care. One way of showing you care is to *pay attention* to people, to what they are doing and to how they are feeling. And if you are clear about the standards you're looking for and you believe and expect that people will perform like winners, then you're going to notice lots of examples of people doing things right.[8]

If you're going to catch people doing things right and doing the right things, you need information and you have to get out from behind your desk to get it. You have to be mobile. You have to spend time with your people and know what they are doing, otherwise your wanderings could be meaningless. In our consulting practice, we developed a methodology of one-on-one sessions that is so simple and yet so powerful if people will follow it. With our long-term clients, we ask the managers to meet with their people for fifteen to thirty minutes once a week, preferably every week. A lot of managers complain that they don't have the time, but even if they had ten people and did a full half hour with each employee, that's only five hours a week. We advise that managers let their direct reports set the agenda. Let your people talk to you about what's important to them. When you do, amazing things will happen. They'll begin to tell you about problems that they need your help with. They'll talk to you about things that are going well that you didn't know about. They'll inform you of things you didn't know about.

You have to make it a high priority to catch people doing things right. At the same time, a good leader must seek balance between performance and morale. I'm a warm, fuzzy type, and sometimes I focus too much on morale, that is, making sure people feel good about themselves. The reality is you also need results. If you can help people perform well within the context of their organizational setting, you accomplish both things. They will feel their absolute best, and the work will be done well. But a delicate balance exists between relationships and results. You can't just go around high-fiving people and expect results.

Exemplary Leaders Personalize Recognition

One of the more familiar complaints Jim and Barry have heard about recognition over their years of research is that it's too often highly predictable, routine, and impersonal. A one-size-fits-all approach to recognition feels contrived, and people can see right through it. Over time it can even backfire, increasing cynicism and actually damaging credibility.

One company president I worked with made a habit of greeting every employee during the holiday season. I told him that was a waste of time. "What do you mean it's a waste of time?" he retorted. "My father always did it."

"Yes, but your father knew everybody, he had a lot fewer people, and he could say something specific about their family," I replied. "You don't know over half the people, a number of them don't even like you, and you're running around wishing them a happy holiday."

He got upset at me for saying that, but the following December proved to be an eye-opener for him. He got sick and couldn't be there for his annual walk-around, so one of his employees got a paper bag, pasted his picture on it, cut some air holes to breathe through, and walked around the company wishing people a happy holiday. Everyone was in hysterics.

Praising without specifics doesn't mean much. When we affirm people, there has to be purpose behind it. That way, the praise is related to what people are trying to accomplish, either personally or organizationally. For example, just saying, "John, you're a wonderful guy" doesn't mean much. It might be true, but it doesn't communicate anything of value to John. If, however, I say, "One of the reasons I really like to be around you is because you're such a good listener," John comes away with specific praise in relation to something he does well.

If you're the kind of leader who looks for the positive things in your people, make sure you give them immediate feedback about it. That way, people will know you're really noticing. When I get back from a long business trip, I ask the key people in our company to tell me which people have done good things while I've been gone. Then I wander around and say, "You know, John, I was just talking to Susan, and she told me about what you did. That's fabulous." Not only does that person get positive feedback from me but their image of their boss gets a boost. One of the best ways to develop good relationships with your people is to let them know you're passing good news up the hierarchy.

If you really want to ignite your people, develop a recognition system based on things they did right. There's nothing worse than getting glittering generalities about something you did, when everyone knows it was just a political deal. But if someone goes out of her way for a customer and somebody else sees that and offers her congratulations, that's meaningful praise.

One thing I'm *not* a big fan of is Employee-of-the-Month contests. In my opinion, Employee-of-the-Month is a "big duck" activity. Committee members are heard saying things like, "Someone from the same department can't win two months in a row, quack quack," or "She's been here for a long time; maybe we ought to recognize her, quack quack." Instead, why not set up Employee-of-the-Moment events that celebrate any time a customer or colleague catches somebody doing something right? Create a "wall of fame" where people can leave notes about what others did well.

Getting caught doing something right makes anyone's day. As a leader who wants to reward good behavior, you can pack a lot more relevance into your reward system by asking a simple question. I always sit down with my people and say, "If I catch you doing something right, what's the best way I could recognize it? Would you like a letter? Should I call your husband or wife? Shall we announce it?" People prefer to be recognized in different ways, so ask them. What motivates people is what motivates people.

For example, you might go to a certain employee and say, "You're doing such a great job I'm going to give you a 10 percent raise." But the reality may be that the person's spouse has a good job, and they already have plenty of money. What he would really like is more responsibility in some other area. Or you go to someone else and say, "You're doing a fabulous job; I'm going to give you the opportunity to do this also." But that person has had an illness in the family and could really use some extra money. Find out what motivates your people best so you can make your rewards relevant.

In our book *Gung Ho!,*[9] Sheldon Bowles and I talk about three leadership principles to boost enthusiasm, increase performance, and achieve astonishing results in any organization. The last of the three principles—the Gift of the Goose—ties in perfectly with this component of encouraging the heart. In short, the Gift of the Goose is cheering others on. Wild geese fly thousands of miles every year. And they do it cheering each other on every step of the way, honking encouragement to one another.

A leader who cheers those around him, offering specific praise for things done right, is a leader who will win the hearts of others and see great things accomplished. In this leadership environment, everybody wins. When that occurs, a leader's heart, head, and hands are all aligned.

THE HABITS

If encouraging the heart is important as a servant leader, and Jesus modeled that, how do we consistently engage in those good servant leader behaviors?

Everyday leaders face hundreds of challenges to their intentions to be servant leaders and to encourage the hearts of others. Our adversary is waiting every day to get us to be ego-driven, to be self-serving. EGO stands for edging God out. The temptations of life, particularly false pride and fear, make it easy for us to edge God out as the focus of our worship, as our source of security and self-worth and as our primary audience and judge. When you start to edge God out in your daily decision making as a leader, the integrity of your leadership is quickly eroded. Every day we must recalibrate our good intentions through five disciplines:

1. *Solitude.* Spending time alone with God.
2. *Prayer.* Speaking with God.
3. *Study of scripture.* Preparing for the challenges that are yet to come.
4. *Faith in God's unconditional love.* Proceeding with confidence grounded in trust.
5. *Involvement in accountability relationships.* Having truth tellers to keep you on track and with whom you can share your vulnerability.

These disciplines permit leaders to ask themselves, "How am I going to be today? Am I going to be self-serving? Or am I going to be a servant?"

Unless servant leaders take care of themselves by practicing habits that recalibrate their commitment to serve rather than be served, life can become a rat race that they have to survive. And the problem with a rat race is that even if you win it, you're still a rat.

In conclusion, leading like Jesus is not about "soft management." Servant leadership makes sense, not just because it is mandated by Jesus but because it is the most effective way to produce a great organization. True greatness only occurs when the heart, head, hands, and habits of a leader are aligned. With that kind of alignment, extraordinary levels of loyalty, trust, and productivity will result; when out of alignment, frustration, mistrust, and diminished long-term productivity are the results.

So lead like Jesus! That's the best way to encourage the heart and get the best results. My prayer is that you will take that first step and allow God to mold you into the leader you were meant to be.

Questions for Reflection

1. How often do I wander around looking for people doing things right and doing the right things? How am I consciously paying attention to people's positive behaviors? How am I making note of them?

2. What have I done recently to recognize someone in my organization in a personal way? How did I determine that the recognition would be meaningful?

3. When was the last instance when I cheered someone in my organization? What behavior was I trying to reward? How specific was I with praise?

4. How often do I take time to encourage my own heart? How aware am I of my own intrinsic worth as a child of God? Do I remember that God loves each person I lead?

FINAL REFLECTIONS

8 LEADERSHIP IS A RELATIONSHIP

James M. Kouzes and Barry Z. Posner

If Jesus had not been able to attract followers, Christianity might never have spread. And it was not just the message that attracted followers; it was the man and his ability to engage with others. This may seem like an obvious point, but it's critical when we're talking about leadership, because the outcome of leadership is a result of the relationship.

Just imagine if Jesus had been the kind of leader the Roman emperors were. Do you really think that over two thousand years later people would be referring to Jesus as a leadership role model? It's not just what he said, it's also *how he behaved* that makes his story significant in the leadership literature.

Leadership is a relationship between those who aspire to lead and those who choose to follow. Sometimes that relationship is one-to-one. Sometimes it's one-to-many. Regardless of the number, in order to thrive in these disquieting times, Christian leaders must master the dynamics of the leadership relationship.

Five strong themes weave together these *Christian Reflections on The Leadership Challenge.* They give us a deeper appreciation for how faith informs and supports leadership, no matter the context. They also demonstrate that Christian leaders have an important contribution to make to our understanding of the dynamics of the leadership relationship. The five key messages we hear repeated in one form or another by all the contributors are these:

1. Credibility is the foundation of leadership.
2. Leadership is personal.
3. Leaders serve.
4. Leaders sacrifice.
5. Leaders keep hope alive.

CREDIBILITY IS THE FOUNDATION OF LEADERSHIP

If leadership is a relationship, then what is the foundation of that relationship? For over two decades and across six continents, we've asked people what they look for and admire in a leader—in someone whose direction they would willingly follow. The key word in this question is *willingly*. In all those years, the response has been the same. The most important personal quality people look for and admire in a leader is personal credibility.[1] *Credibility is the foundation of leadership. If people don't believe in the messenger, they won't believe the message.* This finding has been so consistent for over twenty years that we've come to call it The First Law of Leadership.

And what is credibility behaviorally? We've asked this question thousands of times, and the most frequent response we get is, "Do What You Say You Will Do," or DWYSYWD for short.

Embedded in this behavioral description of credibility are two essentials: *say* and *do*. Leaders must stand for something, believe in something, and care about something. Then they must act on those ideals.

To become a credible leader, as we pointed out in Chapter Two, we each have to first determine what's important to us. Each person has to find his or her voice. This point was underscored by every contributor to this volume. No one was ambiguous about his or her beliefs, and no one was timid about talking about them openly.

Of course, voice and values can be expressed in lots of different ways. Each leader in this book is unique. So are you. Voice and values can be expressed by a businessperson, a volunteer, a parent, a teacher, a missionary, a minister, or by anyone in any role. Voice and values can be expressed on a farm, on a mission, in a coffee business, in a charity, in a classroom, in a church, in a home, or in any place where there are other people. They can be expressed Monday through Friday, as well as on Saturday and Sunday. They can be expressed anytime and anywhere there are human needs to be served.

For Christian leaders, of course, one's voice is also part of a choir—a choir of shared values. Behind the melody there is a beat, and that beat comes from a deeply held set of beliefs about living with integrity, feeding the hungry, serving the poor, aiding the afflicted, and spreading the gospel. It's about doing God's work whatever your calling.

But it's the "do" part of DWYSYWD that seems to elude a lot of would-be leaders and has been forgotten by the fallen ones.

Not too long ago, one of us (Jim) was visiting with David McAllister-Wilson, president of Wesley Theological Seminary in Washington, D.C. (and a contributor to this book). Accompanying Jim was his mom. While waiting for David to return from a meeting, Mary Bates, David's assistant, brought them each a cup of coffee.

Jim reported that as his mom picked up her coffee cup to take a sip, he noticed that inscribed on the side of her cup was a quote that read, "Will the road you're on get you to my place?"—God.

That coffee-cup epiphany in David's office was just one more reminder of how important the credibility lesson is, especially in these disquieting times. *The legacy you leave is the life you lead.* Will the road you're on get you to God's place? After having read all the stories in this book, there is no question that each leader followed a path that was true to his or her values and that each was behaving in ways consistent with Christian principles. None is perfect, and none is a saint, but all took seriously the "Do What You Say You Will Do" message.

LEADERSHIP IS PERSONAL

Because credibility is the foundation, the individual leading is central to any discussion of exemplary leadership. We cannot engage in any serious discussion of the subject in the purely abstract or conceptual. Leadership is personal. It's not about *them*; ultimately it's about *you and me*.

Research on employee engagement clearly supports this message. Surveys from eighty thousand managers in over four hundred companies reveal that it's the *immediate* manager who has more influence on employees' engagement with their work than any other single factor—more important, for example, than pay, benefits, or bonuses.[2] It's the immediate manager who has the most influence on whether a person voluntarily stays or leaves an organization. In other words, people don't quit their organizations; they quit their leaders. Expand this research to religious institutions and you find similar results.[3] The spiritual commitment of congregational members is driven by their congregational engagement, and that engagement is directly related to the kind of leadership they are getting.

The people featured in this book took leadership personally. They realized that they were called to action, and they seized that opportunity. Whether the challenge found them or they found the challenge, they took personal responsibility for doing something about it. However and wherever you express your values and beliefs, *you* have to take leadership personally. Seizing the initiative has absolutely nothing to do with position. It's about attitude and action.

Because leadership is personal, it also means that leadership development is *self*-development. Engineers may have their computers, and painters may have their brushes and canvases, but leaders have only themselves. The instrument of leadership is the self, and the mastery of the art of leadership comes from the mastery of the self.

Self-development is not about stuffing in a whole bunch of new information or trying out the latest technique. It's about leading out of what is already in your soul. It's about liberating the leader within you. It's about setting yourself free.

LEADERS SERVE

It's useful to remember that Jesus was not elected to serve as the formal leader of a movement: "With 51 percent of the popular vote, the winner is Jesus of Nazareth!" Neither did a board of directors get together and select Jesus to be their CEO. He had no formal organizational power to do what he did. He just acted like a leader, and others started to follow and to believe.

In the secular world of leadership, people are so accustomed to saying "leader" and "CEO" in the same breath that they've come to assume the two are equivalent. The same could be said of the church hierarchy. The old command-and-control style of leadership still haunts the corridors of power, and the ghost of ancient practice still has a grip on our psyche. Certainly, CEOs should act like leaders, but the title is not what makes a CEO a leader. Leadership is not about position. It's about practice. Leadership is not conferred. It's earned.

This is another of the consistent messages in this book. Every one of our contributors tells us that leaders serve. We see it in every one of the case examples. Leaders serve a purpose, as do the people who have made it possible for them to lead.[4] They put the guiding principles of the organization ahead of all else and then strive to live by them. They're the first to do what has been agreed upon. The lessons that leadership is a service and that leaders are servants are likely the most significant Christian teachings about the nature of leadership.

The concept of *servant leadership* has been getting more and more attention lately, but it's not new to the secular leadership literature. Over thirty years ago, Robert Greenleaf pointed out that "*the great leader is seen as servant first,* and that simple fact is the key to [the leader's] greatness."[5] Greenleaf, who had spent thirty years as a senior executive in a Fortune 500 company, devoted the last years of his career reflecting on and writing about leadership. He observed that those people who believed foremost in the concept of service, who were servant leaders, were also the most successful. "The best test of this," Greenleaf observed, is

> Do those being served grow as persons? Do they, *while being served,* become healthier, wiser, freer, more autonomous, more likely themselves to become servants? *And,* what is the effect on the least privileged in society; will they benefit, or, at least, not be further deprived?[6]

Greenleaf's teachings have gained currency across the globe, and the fact that they continue to resonate in today's world is testimony to the power of his message. Greenleaf addressed his writings to leaders of all faiths, organizations, and nations. He did not intend it for one exclusive audience. Still, the message of leader-as-servant is clearly one that speaks to the heart of every Christian. The contributors to this book would argue that you cannot be a Christian leader unless you see yourself as servant first. There's no choice here. You either are or you aren't. It comes with the territory.

LEADERS SACRIFICE

Another undercurrent of thought that runs through all of these reflective chapters is the message that leaders must give something up in order to get something more significant. They may give up comfort, wealth, security, time, or even personal safety. What they get is the great joy and satisfaction of knowing that others are the beneficiaries of their service.

Leaders are selfless. Leaders sacrifice, and by sacrificing they demonstrate that they're not in it for themselves; instead, they have the interests of others at heart. When leaders accept that they are servants first, then they clearly know where they stand. And it's not at the head of the line.

This is a far cry from superstar executives who negotiate multi-million-dollar deals and then can walk away rich, even when their companies fail. It's a far cry from those in high office who can get away with stuff the rest of us can't. They may be members of the Christian faith, but their behavior says something else.

Another thing that we've consistently found in our research is that people want leaders who are inspiring, upbeat, and energetic. People want leaders with *passion*. When we think of a passionate person, we think of someone with lots of enthusiasm, excitement, and zeal for their cause. All of this is accurate. But there is more to this word.

When you look up *passion* in the etymological dictionary, you see that it comes from the Greek word for pain and suffering![7]

A passionate person is someone who suffers. A *com*passionate person is someone who suffers *with* others. When we point this out to our students and clients, they quickly get it. It becomes clearer and clearer to them that the leaders who are the most admired are those who have suffered the most, who have sacrificed the most.

This may sound like a very harsh standard to set, but that's not our decision. That was the decision of Christ himself. He made the ultimate sacrifice. Now, we're not prescribing that you carry a cross or wear a crown of thorns to prove you're a good leader. But we are definitely suggesting that leadership requires a willingness to make personal sacrifices for the sake of a higher purpose.

There's a very positive consequence to selfless action. When leaders are selfless and humble, people are much more inclined to trust them. Putting others first—and meaning it—will earn you more credibility than if you try to place yourself at the head of the line.

LEADERS KEEP HOPE ALIVE

We're only a few years into this new millennium, and we've already experienced extremely disquieting economic, political, and social upheavals. The forecasts are still pretty gloomy. But just because the clouds have obscured the view doesn't mean there is no sun. That's how exemplary leaders see it, anyway. When you review the cases in this book, you'll see an abundance of adversity in each situation. It could have discouraged our leaders from continuing their quests. But they weren't; instead, they kept hope alive.

Christian leaders know that service and sacrifice are redemptive. They know that there is a deeper reward when you make sacrifices for the sake of a higher purpose and in service of others. They know that a potent antidote to the increased cynicism and stresses of our time is renewed faith in human capacity and an intensely optimistic belief that together we will overcome.

Leaders keep hope alive. They keep hope alive by demonstrating the courage of their convictions. They keep hope alive by painting positive images of the future. They keep hope alive by taking charge of change. They keep hope alive by trusting the abilities of others. They keep hope alive by recognizing the dedication of others as they get extraordinary things done.

Hope is attitude in action. It enables people to mobilize their healing and their achieving powers. It helps them to transcend the difficulties of today and envision the potentialities of tomorrow. Hope enables people to find the will and the way to aspire to greatness. Hope is testimony to the power of the human spirit. Leadership is often a struggle, and the only way to thrive is to keep hope alive.

In the final analysis, there is no shortage of opportunities to lead. There is no shortage of opportunities to make a difference in the world—be that world your family, neighborhood, congregation, school, or corporation. Challenge is the opportunity for greatness, and leaders seize these opportunities to make a difference.

The most significant contributions leaders make are not to today's bottom line but to the long-term development of people and institutions that adapt, prosper, and grow. The next time you say to yourself, "Why don't *they* do something about this?" look in the mirror. Ask the person you see, "Why don't *you* do something about this?"

NOTES

CHAPTER ONE

1. J. M. Kouzes and B. Z. Posner, *The Leadership Practices Inventory* (San Francisco: Pfeiffer, 2003). For information on The Leadership Practices, visit www.leadershipchallenge.com.
2. The Five Practices of Exemplary Leadership® is a registered trademark of J. M. Kouzes and B. Z. Posner. All rights reserved. For an extensive discussion of The Five Practices, see Kouzes and Posner, *The Leadership Challenge* (San Francisco: Jossey-Bass, 2003).
3. J. C. Maxwell, *The 21 Irrefutable Laws of Leadership: Follow Them and People Will Follow You* (Nashville, Tenn.: Thomas Nelson, 1998).
4. P. Lencioni. *The Five Temptations of a CEO* (San Francisco: Jossey-Bass, 1998).
5. K. Blanchard and S. Johnson, *The One Minute Manager* (New York: William Morrow, 1982).

CHAPTER TWO

1. You can access summaries of this research by visiting our Web site, www.leadershipchallenge.com. Go to the "Guide to the Research" section, and you'll see a number of research summaries under the heading "Religious."

CHAPTER THREE

1. J. M. Kouzes and B. Z. Posner, *The Leadership Challenge* (San Francisco: Jossey-Bass, 2002), 54.

CHAPTER FOUR

1. M. L. King Jr., "I've Been to the Mountaintop." Speech delivered in support of the striking sanitation workers at Mason Temple in Memphis, Tennessee, on April 3, 1968. Reprinted by arrangement with the Estate of Martin Luther King Jr., c/o Writers House as agent for the proprietor of New York, New York. Copyright 1968 Dr. Martin Luther King Jr., copyright renewed 1991 Coretta Scott King.

2. B. Shore, *The Cathedral Within* (New York: Random House, 1999).
3. Conversation with Beecher Hicks on May 16, 2003.
4. Sept. 11, 2001, Fairlington United Methodist Church.
5. J. M. Kouzes and B. Z. Posner, *The Leadership Challenge* (San Francisco: Jossey-Bass, 2002), 143.
6. L. H. Weems Jr., *Church Leadership: Vision, Team, Culture, and Integrity* (Nashville: Abingdon Press, 1993), 58.
7. Weems, "There Is Still a Vision." Speech to the General Council on Ministries, United Methodist Church, Dayton, Ohio, October 23, 1992.
8. L. Russell, "A Song for You," from the album *Leon Russell Shelter,* A&M Records, 1970.
9. Fairlington United Methodist Church treasurer's report.
10. Bishop J. K. Matthews, telling of his conversation with Gandhi.

CHAPTER FIVE

1. Kouzes and Posner, *The Leadership Challenge,* 2002, 184.
2. Kouzes and Posner, *The Leadership Challenge,* 2002, 129.
3. J. Collins, *Why Some Companies Make the Leap and Others Don't* (New York: HarperCollins, 2001).
4. Kouzes and Posner, *The Leadership Challenge,* 2002, 201.
5. Kouzes and Posner, *The Leadership Challenge,* 2002, 214.
6. Kouzes and Posner, *The Leadership Challenge,* 2002, 233.
7. Kouzes and Posner, *The Leadership Challenge,* 2002, 229–230.
8. Kouzes and Posner, *The Leadership Challenge,* 2002, 230.

CHAPTER SIX

1. Kouzes and Posner, *The Leadership Challenge,* 2002, 18, 242.
2. Kouzes and Posner, *The Leadership Challenge,* 2002, 248.
3. M. Novak, *Business as a Calling: Work and the Examined Life* (New York: Free Press, 1996).

CHAPTER SEVEN

1. Blanchard and Johnson, *The One Minute Manager,* 1982.
2. G. MacDonald, *Ordering Your Private World* (Nashville, Tenn.: Thomas Nelson, 2003).
3. J. Collins, *Good to Great,* 2001.
4. K. Blanchard and J. Stoner, *Full Steam Ahead!* (San Francisco: Berrett-Koehler, 2003).
5. Kouzes and Posner, *The Leadership Challenge,* 2002, 318.
6. Blanchard and Johnson, *The One Minute Manager,* 1982.
7. K. Blanchard and R. Lorber, *Putting the One Minute Manager to Work* (New York: Penguin, Putnam, 1998).

8. Kouzes and Posner, *The Leadership Challenge,* 2002, 327.
9. K. Blanchard and S. Bowles, *Gung Ho!* (New York: William Morrow, 1998).

Other books by Ken Blanchard include:

K. Blanchard and P. Hodges, *The Servant Leader* (Nashville, Tenn.: J. Countryman, 2003).

K. Blanchard and S. T. Cathy, *The Generosity Factor* (Grand Rapids, Mich.: Zondervan, 2002).

K. Blanchard, T. Lacinak, C. Tompkins, and J. Ballard, *Whale Done!* (New York: Simon & Schuster, 2002).

K. Blanchard, B. Hybels, and P. Hodges, *Leadership by the Book* (New York: William Morrow, 1999).

CHAPTER EIGHT

1. For a current summary of our research on credibility, see J. M. Kouzes and B. Z. Posner, *The Leadership Challenge* (San Francisco: Jossey-Bass, 2002), 23–39. Also see J. M. Kouzes and B. Z. Posner, *Credibility: How Leaders Gain and Lose It, Why People Demand It* (San Francisco: Jossey-Bass, 2003).
2. M. Buckingham and C. Coffman, *First, Break All the Rules: What the World's Greatest Managers Do Differently* (New York: Simon & Schuster, 1999), 34.
3. For more on The Gallup Organization's research on religion and values, visit www.gallup.com. See especially, A. L. Winseman's, *The Driving Factor Behind Spiritual Health, The Gallup Tuesday Briefing,* July 9, 2002.
4. See Kouzes and Posner, *Credibility,* 183–217.
5. R. K. Greenleaf, *Servant Leadership: A Journey Into the Nature of Legitimate Power and Greatness* (New York: Paulist Press, 1977), 1. For extensive information on the life and writings of R. K. Greenleaf, contact The Greenleaf Center for Servant-Leadership on the Web at www.greenleaf.org. Interested readers may also enjoy J. A. Autry's *The Servant Leader: How to Build a Creative Team, Develop Morale, and Improve Bottom-Line Performance* (Roseville, Calif.: Prima Publishing, 2001).
6. Greenleaf, *Servant Leadership,* 13–14.
7. E. Partridge, *Origins: A Short Etymological Dictionary of Modern English* (New York: Macmillan, 1977), 75.

SELECTED READINGS ON LEADERSHIP

GENERAL LEADERSHIP

Warren Bennis, *On Becoming a Leader*. Reading, Mass: Perseus, 1994.

James MacGregor Burns, *Leadership*. New York: HarperCollins, 1978.

Jim Collins, *Good to Great: Why Some Companies Make the Leap and Others Don't*. New York: HarperCollins, 2001.

Howard Gardner, *Leading Minds: An Anatomy of Leadership*. New York: Basic Books, 1995.

John Gardner, *On Leadership*. New York: Free Press, 1990.

James M. Kouzes and Barry Z. Posner, *The Leadership Challenge*. San Francisco: Jossey-Bass, 2002.

John C. Maxwell, *The 21 Irrefutable Laws of Leadership: Follow Them and People Will Follow You*. Nashville, Tenn.: Thomas Nelson, 1998.

Edgar H. Schein, *Organizational Culture and Leadership*. (2nd ed.) San Francisco: Jossey-Bass, 1992.

Lovett H. Weems Jr., *Take the Next Step: Leading Lasting Change in the Church*. Nashville, Tenn.: Abington Press, 2003.

MODEL THE WAY

David Batstone, *Saving the Corporate Soul and (Who Knows?) Maybe Your Own*. San Francisco: Jossey-Bass, 2003.

James M. Kouzes and Barry Z. Posner, *Credibility: How Leaders Gain and Lose It, Why People Demand It*. San Francisco: Jossey-Bass, 1993. (Paperback version 2003.)

Max De Pree, *Leadership Is an Art*. New York: Doubleday, 1989.

Robert K. Greenleaf, *Servant Leadership: A Journey Into Legitimate Power and Greatness*. Paulist Press, 1983.

Charles C. Manz, *The Leadership Wisdom of Jesus: Practical Lessons for Today*. San Francisco: Berrett-Koehler, 1999.

John C. Maxwell, *Running with Giants: What Old Testament Heroes Want You to Know about Life and Leadership*. New York: Warner Books, 2003.

Michael Novak, *Business as a Calling: Work and the Examined Life*. New York: Free
    Press, 1996.
Parker J. Palmer, *Let Your Life Speak: Listening to the Voice of Vocation*. San Francisco:
    Jossey-Bass, 2000.
Terry Pearce, *Leading Out Loud: Inspiring Change Through Authentic Communica-
    tions*. (rev. ed.) San Francisco: Jossey-Bass, 2003.

INSPIRE A SHARED VISION

Boyd Clarke and Ron Crossland, *The Leader's Voice: How Your Communication Can
    Inspire Action and Get Results!* New York: Select Books, 2002.
Gary Hamel, *Leading the Revolution*. Boston: Harvard Business School Press, 2000.
Jennifer James, *Thinking in the Future Tense: Leadership Skills for the New Age*. New
    York: Simon & Schuster, 1996.
Richard J. Leider and David A. Shapiro, *Whistle While You Work: Heeding Your Life's
    Calling*. San Francisco: Berrett-Koehler, 2001.
Burt Nanus, *Visionary Leadership*. San Francisco: Jossey-Bass, 1992.
Peter Schwartz, *The Art of the Long View*. New York: Currency, 1991.
Andy Stanley, *Visioneering: God's Blueprint for Developing and Maintaining Personal
    Vision*. Sisters, Ore.: Multnomah Publishers, 1999.
Bruce Sterling, *Tomorrow Now: Envisioning the Next Fifty Years*. New York: Random
    House, 2003.
Margaret Wheatley, *Leadership and the New Science*. San Francisco: Berrett-Koehler,
    1992.

CHALLENGE THE PROCESS

Arlene Blum, *Annapurna: A Woman's Place, Twentieth Anniversary Edition*. San Fran-
    cisco: Sierra Club Books, 1998.
Mihaly Csikszentmihalyi, *Finding Flow: The Psychology of Engagement with Everyday
    Life*. New York: Basic Books, 1997.
Richard Farson and Ralph Keyes, *Whoever Makes the Most Mistakes Wins: The Para-
    dox of Innovation*. New York: Free Press, 2002.
Ronald Heifitz and Marty Linsky, *Leadership on the Line: Staying Alive through the
    Dangers of Leading*. Boston: Harvard Business School Press, 2002.
Richard Foster and Sarah Kaplan, *Creative Destruction: Why Companies that Are Built
    to Last Underperform the Market—and How to Successfully Transform Them*.
    New York: Currency, 2001.
Tom Kelley, with Jonathon Littman, *The Art of Innovation: Lessons in Creativity from
    IDEO, America's Leading Design Firm*. New York: Currency Doubleday, 2001.
Patrick Lencioni, *The Five Temptations of a CEO*. San Francisco: Jossey-Bass, 1998.
Louis Patler, *Tilt! Irreverent Lessons for Leading Innovation in the New Economy*.
    Oxford, England: Capstone, 1999.

ENABLE OTHERS TO ACT

Michael Abrashoff, *It's Your Ship: Management Techniques from the Best Damn Ship in the Navy.* New York: Warner, 2002.

Ken Blanchard, John Carlos, and Alan Randolph, *The Three Keys to Empowerment.* San Francisco: Berrett-Koehler, 1999.

Peter Block, *The Empowered Manager: Positive Political Skills at Work.* San Francisco: Jossey-Bass, 1987. (Paperback version 1991.)

Marcus Buckingham and Curt Coffman, *First, Break all the Rules: What the World's Greatest Managers Do Differently.* New York: Simon & Schuster, 1999.

Roger Fisher and William Ury, *Getting to Yes.* New York: Penguin, 1988.

Malcolm Gladwell, *The Tipping Point: How Little Things Make a Big Difference.* Boston: Little, Brown, 2002.

Daniel Goleman, *Working with Emotional Intelligence.* New York: Bantam, 1998.

Charles A. O'Reilly and Jeffrey Pfeffer, *Hidden Value: How Great Companies Achieve Extraordinary Results with Ordinary People.* Boston: Harvard Business School Press, 2000.

Jack Stack and Bo Burlingham, *A Stake in the Outcome: Building a Culture of Ownership for the Long-Term Success of Your Business.* New York: Currency Doubleday, 2002.

ENCOURAGE THE HEART

Ken Blanchard, Thad Lacinak, Chuck Tompkins, and Jim Ballard, *Whale Done! The Power of Positive Relationships.* New York: Free Press, 2002.

Terrence Deal and M. K. Deal, *Corporate Celebrations: Play, Purpose, and Profit at Work.* San Francisco: Berrett-Koehler, 1998.

Adrian Gostick and Chester Elton, *Managing with Carrots: Using Recognition to Attract and Retain the Best People.* Layton, Utah: Gibbs Smith, 2001.

Dave Hemsath and Leslie Yerkes, *301 Ways to Have Fun at Work.* San Francisco: Berrett-Koehler, 1997.

James M. Kouzes and Barry Z. Posner, *Encouraging the Heart: A Leader's Guide to Rewarding and Recognizing Others.* San Francisco: Jossey-Bass, 1999. (Paperback version 2003.)

Bob Nelson, *1001 Ways to Reward Employees.* New York: Workman, 1994.

ACKNOWLEDGMENTS

We have been writing as a team for over twenty years. Each time we begin a project, we know that one of the many joys of the process is the opportunity to work with scores of engaging, dedicated, and talented people. We keep learning and relearning that collaboration is a virtue to be cherished. This is especially true for *Christian Reflections on The Leadership Challenge* because this is the first time we've had the chance to serve as editors of a volume in which others have written so eloquently about our model. We are deeply honored to be in their company.

We are profoundly grateful to five individuals who devoted countless hours to reflecting upon and recording their thoughts on the meaning of The Five Practices of Exemplary Leadership® in the context of the Christian faith. You will have the pleasure of reading what they have to say in this book, but we had the additional privilege of working with them for over a year. Thank you John Maxwell, David McAllister-Wilson, Pat Lencioni, Nancy Ortberg, and Ken Blanchard. You have enriched our understanding of leadership and have enriched our lives.

One of the trademarks of all our books is the inclusion of numerous cases of *real* people doing *real* things in *real* organizations. These aren't the famous people that you typically read about—you know, the ones who make the covers of the business press. But to us, all the individuals in this book—and all our books—have made a meaningful and memorable contribution to the betterment of our world. Each is an exemplary role model for us all. Their actions are the equal of any leader you'll ever meet, and they are the stars of this book. Thank you to Betty Beene, Lillas Brown, Monte Campbell, Walt Griffin, Adam Hamilton, Ken Horne, Michael Joseph, and John Sage for sharing your stories with us.

We are also grateful to interviewees Anita Burke, Andre Delbecq, Phyllis Jelley, Bob Munce, and Lovett Weems, whose insights on the practices of Christian leaders guided us in our writing. Colleagues Bob Anderson, David Batstone, and Laura Nash also took great care in nominating case examples for us to examine.

Not one word of *Christian Reflections on The Leadership Challenge* would ever have been written, however, if it had not been for John Maxwell and his colleagues at INJOY. John asked us if he could use The Five Practices model as the organizing framework for one of his Catalyst Conferences, and that gracious invitation began the journey that resulted in this book. Thanks to Akemi Cole, Linda Eggers, Tricia Gleghorn, Joy Grubbs, Kevin Small, and the other enthusiastic members of the INJOY organization. We can always count on them to uplift our spirits.

Writer Angie Kiesling deserves special praise for her talents in interviewing and in transforming the spoken word into the written text. Without Angie's genius for the craft of storytelling, this book would never have gotten the kick-start that it needed. Marcia Ford also contributed a brilliant case on one leader's challenge to restore confidence in an organization on the brink, and she helped research biblical scripture for the epigraphs that appear at the beginning of the five leadership practice chapters.

We've worked with JoAnn Johnson on several of our book projects. Among her many gifts are well-tuned ears and adroit fingers; she can take hours of interviews and turn them into scores of transcript pages on a schedule that would be impossible for most mortals. We don't know how she does it, but we are very grateful to her for always moving us forward.

We've collaborated with our publisher, Jossey-Bass, on all our leadership books, instruments, and workbooks. We believe they are the preeminent publisher of leadership books, and it is their awesomely talented group of editors and staff that makes them the envy of the industry. Our editor for this book, Julianna Gustafson, combines dogged persistence with gentle patience and towering competence with empowering encouragement. The fact that this book actually made it to press is testimony to her belief in the worth of this project and to her amazing ability to work with others. Although we and the other authors may have written the chapters, Julianna had to shepherd this project from start to finish, and that was, as everyone involved knows, a remarkable feat. Working alongside her was Catherine Craddock, who conducted interviews and secured permissions to publish the cases. Mary Garrett was our production editor, and she worked magic—she made a book appear where there was once an electronic manuscript. Sandy Siegle, Erik Thrasher, Michael Cook, and other members of the Jossey-Bass team all made significant contributions behind the scenes to navigate the intricacies of helping this book reach its audience.

Blessings to each and every one of you.

Santa Clara, California   Jim Kouzes
January 2004   Barry Posner

ABOUT THE AUTHORS

James M. Kouzes and **Barry Z. Posner** coauthored the award-winning and best-selling book *The Leadership Challenge* (2002). In addition, they coauthored *Credibility: How Leaders Gain It and Lose It, Why People Demand It* (1993, 2003), which was chosen by *Industry Week* as one of that year's five best management books, as well as *Encouraging the Heart* (1999, 2003), *The Leadership Challenge Journal* (2003), and *The Leadership Challenge Workbook* (2003). Jim and Barry also developed the highly acclaimed *Leadership Practices Inventory* (LPI), a 360-degree questionnaire assessing leadership behavior; the LPI is one of the most widely used leadership assessment instruments in the world. More than two hundred doctoral dissertations and academic research projects have been based on The Five Practices of Exemplary Leadership® model. CRM Learning has produced a number of leadership and management development videos based on their publications.

Jim and Barry were named by the International Management Council as the recipients of the prestigious Wilbur M. McFeely Award in 2001. This honor puts them in the company of Ken Blanchard, Stephen Covey, Peter Drucker, Edward Deming, Francis Hesselbein, Lee Iacocca, Rosabeth Moss Kanter, Norman Vincent Peale, and Tom Peters—previous recipients of the award. Jim and Barry are frequent conference speakers, and each has conducted leadership development programs for hundreds of organizations, including Alcoa, Applied Materials, ARCO, AT&T, Australia Post, Bank of America, Bose, Charles Schwab, Cisco Systems, Community Leadership Association,

Conference Board of Canada, Consumers Energy, Dell Computer, Deloitte & Touche, Egon Zehnder International, Federal Express, Gymboree, Hewlett-Packard, IBM, Johnson & Johnson, Kaiser Foundation Health Plans and Hospitals, Lawrence Livermore National Labs, Levi Strauss & Co., L. L. Bean, 3M, Merck, Mervyn's, Motorola, Network Appliance, Roche Bioscience, Siemens, Sun Microsystems, TRW, Toyota, U.S. Postal Service, United Way, and VISA.

Jim Kouzes is an Executive Fellow at the Center for Innovation and Entrepreneurship at the Leavey School of Business, Santa Clara University. He is also chairman emeritus of the Tom Peters Company, a professional services firm that inspires organizations to invent the new world of work using leadership training and consulting solutions. Jim is featured as one of the workplace experts in George Dixon's book *What Works at Work: Lessons from the Masters* (1988) and in *Learning Journeys: Top Management Experts Share Hard-Earned Lessons on Becoming Great Mentors and Leaders,* edited by Marshall Goldsmith, Beverly Kaye, and Ken Shelton (2000). Not only is he a highly regarded leadership scholar and an experienced executive, the *Wall Street Journal* has cited him as one of the twelve most requested non-university executive education providers to U.S. companies. A popular seminar and conference speaker, Jim shares his insights about the leadership practices that contribute to high performance in individuals and organizations.

Jim directed the Executive Development Center (EDC) at Santa Clara University from 1981 through 1987. Under his leadership, the EDC was awarded two gold medals from the Council for the Advancement and Support of Education. He also founded the Joint Center for Human Services Development at San Jose State University, which he managed from 1972 until 1980; prior to that, he was on the staff of the University of Texas School of Social Work.

His career in training and development began in 1969, when, as part of the Southwest urban team, Jim conducted seminars for Community Action Agency staff and volunteers in the "war on poverty" effort. Jim received his B.A. degree (1967) with honors from Michigan State University in political science and a certificate (1974) from San Jose State University's School of Business for completion of the internship in organization development.

Jim's interest in leadership began while he was growing up in Washington, D.C. In 1961, he was one of a dozen Eagle Scouts selected to serve in John F. Kennedy's Honor Guard at the presidential inauguration. Inspired by Kennedy, he served as a Peace Corps volunteer from 1967 through 1969. Jim can be reached at jim@kouzesposner.com.

Barry Posner is dean of The Leavey School of Business and Professor of Leadership at Santa Clara University (Silicon Valley, California), where he has received numerous teaching and innovation awards, including his school's and his university's highest faculty awards. An internationally renowned scholar and educator, Barry is the author or coauthor of more than one hundred research and practitioner-focused articles in such publications as *Academy of Management Journal, Journal of Applied Psychology, Human Relations, Personnel Psychology, IEEE Transactions on Engineering Management, Journal of Business Ethics, California Management Review, Business Horizons,* and *Management Review.* In addition to the books he coauthored with Jim Kouzes, Barry has coauthored several books on project management, most recently *Checkered Flag Projects: 10 Rules for Creating and Managing Projects that Win!* Barry is on the editorial review boards for the *Journal of Management Inquiry* and *Journal of Business Ethics.*

Barry received his B.A. degree (1970) with honors from the University of California, Santa Barbara, in political science. He received his M.A. degree (1972) from The Ohio State University in public administration and his Ph.D. degree (1976) from the University of Massachusetts, Amherst, in organizational behavior and administrative theory.

Having consulted with a wide variety of public and private sector organizations around the globe, Barry currently sits on the board of directors for the American Institute of Architects (AIA) and the San Jose Repertory Theatre. He has served previously on the boards of Public Allies, Big Brothers/Big Sisters of Santa Clara County, the Center for Excellence in Non-Profits, Sigma Phi Epsilon Fraternity, and several start-up companies. At Santa Clara University, he has served as associate dean for graduate programs and managing partner for the Executive Development Center.

Barry's interest in leadership began when he was a student during the turbulent unrest on college campuses in the late 1960s; he was participating in and reflecting on the effort to understand the balance between energetic collective action and chaotic and frustrated anarchy. Barry can be reached at bposner@scu.edu.

More information about Jim and Barry and their work can be found on their Web site: www.theleadershipchallenge.com.

Ken Blanchard is the cofounder and chief spiritual officer of The Ken Blanchard Companies, a global leader in workplace learning, employee productivity, and leadership effectiveness. He is the coauthor of *The One Minute Manager, Raving Fans, Gung Ho!, Whale Done!* and numerous other best-sellers. His two coauthored books on spirituality in the workplace—*Leadership by the Book* and *The Servant Leader*—are giving new meaning to the important concept of servant leadership. Ken is the cofounder of the Center for Faith-Walk Leadership—a ministry dedicated to helping people lead like Jesus. For more information about FaithWalk, please visit their Web site at www.faithwalkleadership.com.

Patrick Lencioni is the best-selling author of leadership fables, including *The Five Dysfunctions of a Team, The Five Temptations of a CEO,* and *Death By Meeting.* As president and founder of The Table

Group, Pat speaks to and consults with thousands of leaders and organizations each year. The Table Group—a management consulting firm based in the San Francisco Bay Area—specializes in executive team development and organizational health, and provides a variety of services, including consulting, presenting workshops, speaking, and conducting on-line assessments for teams. Pat lives in the Bay Area with his wife, Laura, and their three sons Matthew, Connor, and Casey. He is proud to be a member of the national board of directors of the Make-A-Wish Foundation.

John C. Maxwell speaks in person to hundreds of thousands of people each year. He has communicated his leadership principles to Fortune 500 companies, the U.S. Military Academy at West Point, and sports organizations such as the NCAA, the NBA, and the NFL. Maxwell is the founder of several organizations, including Maximum Impact—an organization that is dedicated to helping people reach their leadership potential. He is the author of more than thirty books, including *Thinking for a Change, There's No Such Thing as Business Ethics,* and *The 21 Irrefutable Laws of Leadership,* which has sold more than one million copies.

David McAllister-Wilson is the president of Wesley Theological Seminary, one of the nation's largest and leading theological schools, preparing approximately 1,300 men and women for ministry every year. He has focused his preaching and speaking in an effort to help revitalize the Mainline Protestant Church, helping to encourage men and women to consider God's call to ministry, and preparing them for leadership. With a strong interest in and focus on leadership development, particularly in local congregations, he helped to establish the G. Douglass Lewis Center for Church Leadership at Wesley. David is married to Drema McAllister-Wilson, who currently serves as pastor of Fairlington United Methodist Church in Alexandria, Virginia. They have three children: Dan, Ashley, and Carter.

Nancy Ortberg is a teaching pastor at Willow Creek Community Church in South Barrington, Illinois. She currently serves as director of the Axis Ministry, for the "eighteen-to-twenty-something" generation. Nancy speaks domestically and internationally to churches on issues of leadership, community, and the next generation. She and her husband, John, have three children: Laura, Mallory, and John.

INDEX

questions on, 81; risk and risk taking in, 24–26, 69, 79–81; search for opportunities and, 22–24, 69; selfless service and, 72–75, 81; stories of Christian leaders who, 19–22, 73–74; teams for, 78–81; willingness to suffer and, 71–72, 75–78

Change: Challenge the Process and, 2, 19–26, 69, 71–81; for change's sake, 74–75; of minds and hearts and actions, 67; of oneself first, 42–46; spirit and, 67–68; team makeup and, 78–79

Character development, 94–95, 122

Charlie Brown and Lucy, 43

Cheering others on, 114–115

Chief executive officer (CEO), 123

Christian leaders. *See* Leaders; Leaders, examples of Christian

Christian leadership. *See* Leadership

Christian Reflections on The Leadership Challenge (Kouzes and Posner): origins of, 3–4; overview of, 4–6

Christian symbols, 65–66

Christianity: as group activity, 59; relational leadership and, 119

Church, the: congregational engagement in, 122; leadership in, 55–56, 59–60; mission in, 62; preaching in, 59–61; vision and revitalization of, 59

Claiborne, S., 86–87

Coaching, performance, 110–111

Coffee company and mission, 13–17

Collaboration: elements of, 28–29; Enable Others to Act and, 26–30, 83, 86–98; fostering, 28–29, 83, 88–90; trust and, 28, 83, 89–90

Collins, J., 78, 104

Commitment: encouraging others with, 103; leadership development and, 94–95, 122

Commitments of leadership, 37

Community spirit, 99

Compassion, 125

Compensation, 114

Competence, development and, 94–95

Compliance, 96–97

Conflicts, value, 107–108

Congressmen, U.S., 74–75

Continuous improvement, 23

1 Corinthians, 1:23, 65

2 Corinthians, 12:9, 41

Corpus, 56

Costa Rica mission, 13–17

Creativity and innovation: Challenge the Process and, 19–20, 23–26; experimentation and, 22–24; seeking opportunities and, 22–24

Credibility: in leadership relationship, 120–121; leading oneself and, 44

Crises, leadership in, 80

Critical incidents, 13

Criticism, faith and, 21–22

Cross, symbol of the, 65

Crucifixion, 65, 75–76, 88–89

Customer-contact people, 109

Customers, as sources of improvement ideas, 23

Cynicism, 19, 96–97, 112–113, 125

Cynics, 19

Dacor, 44–46, 47–48

Daniel 5, 62

David, Samuel's choosing of, 93–94

Davis, L., 64

Day of Atonement, 88

Day-to-day coaching, 110–111

De Pree, M., 90, 95

Dearnley, C., 13–17

Decision making: participatory, in vision sharing, 63–64; strengthening others in, 30

Derrick, J., 60

Development of others, 94–95, 110–115. *See also* Enable Others to Act; Leadership development

Difference, desire to make a, 18, 71–72, 126

Dignity of work, 97

Disciples, 67; leadership development of, 87–88, 101–102; as servant leaders, 101–102; as students, 62

Disciplines, 66, 114–115

Disney, W., 107–108

"Do What You Say You Will Do" (DWYSYWD), 120–121

Driven people, 104–105

Ecclesiastes 2:10, 101

Ego: desire for recognition and, 72, 104–105, 106; giving away power and, 91–98; selfless service *versus* serving, 72–75, 81, 103–105, 110–111, 115

Emergency room doctors, 90–91

Employee engagement, 122

Employee-of-the-Moment events, 114

Employee-of-the-Month contests, 114

Empowerment. *See* Enable Others to Act; Power, sharing and giving away

Enable Others to Act, 2, 26–30, 83, 85–98; Christian reflections on, 5–6, 26–30, 85–98; commitments of, 37; fostering collaboration and, 28–29, 83, 88–90; Jesus' model of, 87–88; overview of, 26–30; power sharing/giving away and, 29–30, 83, 87–88, 88, 90–98; priesthood of all believers concept and, 88–89; readings on, 133; reflection questions for, 98; servant leadership and, 87–88, 96–98; stories of Christian leaders who, 26–30, 85–87, 91–93, 94–95, 96–97; strengthening others and, 29–30, 83, 90–98; talent radar for, 93–94

Enactment, 13

Encourage the Heart, 2, 30–38, 99, 101–116; celebration to, 36, 38, 99; Christian reflections on, 6, 30–38, 101–116; commitments of, 37; habits domain of, 103, 115–116; hands domain of, 103, 110–115; head domain of, 103, 106–109; heart domain of, 103–106; internal and external domains of, 103; overview of, 30–38; performance improvement and, 110–115; readings on, 131; recognizing contributions and, 34–35, 99, 103–105, 106; reflection questions on, 116; results and, 110–115; self-serving *versus* servant leaders and, 103–105, 110–111, 115–116; servant leadership and, 101–116; standards and, 108–109; stories of Christians who, 30–38

Enlisting others, 18–19, 53; in challenge, 78–81; Christian reflections on, 59–68; fishing with a net and, 59–61; keeping an eye on the horizon and, 61–62; listening and, 62–64; preaching and, 59–61

Enthusiasm, 19; challenge and, 25

Envisioning the future, 17–18; Christian reflections on, 56–59; rainbow quality in, 57–59; suffering as catalyst for, 56–57

Epic tales, 59, 66

Equip, 5

ESL and Immigrant Ministries, 26–30

Evangelism: changing oneself *versus*, 43–44; one-on-one, 43–44, 96

Example setting, 11–13, 39, 48–52

Executives, superstar, 123, 124

Exemplary leadership. *See* Five Practices of Exemplary Leadership; Leadership; Stories of exemplary leaders

Exodus 18:18, 21–22, 85

Expectations: performance coaching and, 110–111; power of high, 34–35; recognition for contributions and, 34–35

Experimentation, 24–26, 69

Face-to-face interaction, collaboration and, 30

Failure: expectations for, 34; learning from, 79–81

Faith: during difficult times, 21–22; hope and, 125–126; leadership with, 59; role models for, 51–52; sacrifice and, 65; sharing, one-on-one, 43–44, 96

Fear, 115

Feedback: to Encourage the Heart, 113; selfless *versus* self-serving reactions to, 105

Feeling good, results and, 110, 112

Feet washing, 109

Fishing with a net, 59–61

Five Practices of Exemplary Leadership, 7–38; Christian reflections on, background of, 3–4; Christian reflections on, overview of, 5–6; efficacy of, 7–8; interdependencies among, 6; listed, 2, 37; overview of, 7–38; Ten Commitments and, 37. *See also* Challenge the Process; Enable Others to Act; Encourage the Heart; Inspire a Shared Vision; Model the Way

Five Temptations of a CEO, The (Lencioni), 5

Followers: importance of credibility to, 120; leadership relationship and, 119–126

Following the leader, 48–51

Food outreach ministry, 8–10

Forsythe, G., 16

Frontline employees, 23, 109

Frustration, keeping an eye on the horizon and, 61–62

Full Steam Ahead! (Blanchard and Stoner), 107

Fuller, L., 58

Fuller, M., 58

Fuller Seminary, 95

Gandhi, I., 65

Gandhi, M., 65

Gift of the Goose, 114–115

Gifts of talent: developing others', 94–95; finding others', 93–94

Giving, sacrifice and, 64–65

Gleaning ministry, 9, 10

Goals, 17, 108–109. *See also* Vision
God: EGO and, 115; groundedness in, 106, 115; honoring, in values statement, 45–46
Golden Rule, 42
Good to Great (Collins), 78, 104
Grace, 65
Gratitude, 65
Great commandments, 108
Great Commission, 52
Greenleaf, R. K., 123–124
Griffin, W., 49–51
Gung Ho! (Blanchard and Bowles), 114–115

Habitat for Humanity, 33, 58
Habits domain, of encouraging others, 103, 115–116
Hamilton, A., 30–34
Hands domain, of encouraging others, 103, 110–115
Hardiness, psychological, 25, 77–78
Harvard Business School, 13–14
Harvest of Hope, 10
Head domain, of encouraging others, 103, 106–109
Heart: encouraging others from, 103–106; leading from the, 96–98. *See also* Encourage the Heart
Hebrews, 88; 10:24, 85; 13:7, 41
Hero leader myth, 28
Hero stories, 95–96
Hicks, B., 58
Hierarchical leadership, 109, 110, 111, 123
Holy Spirit, 67, 78, 89
Hope, 57, 125–126
Horizon, keeping an eye on, 61–62
Horne, K., 8–10, 11
"Hour of Power," 102
Hubbard, D. A., 95
Humiliation, public, 75–76, 77
Humility, 71–72; selfless leadership and, 72–75, 81, 104–105
Hunger, story of ministry to, 8–10
Hurricane Andrew, 64
Hybels, B., 92

IBM, 16
Illinois Youth Correctional (IYC) facility, 95–96
Implementation, organizational structure and, 109
Incremental improvement and successes, 80–81
Influence, openness to, 28, 30, 89–90

Initiative, seizing the, 22–24
INJOY, 3–4, 5, 52
Innovation. *See* Creativity and innovation
Inspiration, 18–19
Inspire a Shared Vision, 2, 13–19, 53, 55–68; Christian reflections on, 5, 13–19, 55–68; commitments of, 37; enlisting others and, 18–19, 53, 59–68; envisioning the future and, 17–18, 56–59; fishing with a net and, 59–61; giving life to a vision and, 65–68; keeping an eye on the horizon and, 61–62; overview of, 13–19, 53; readings on, 132; reflection questions on, 68; sacrifice and, 64–65; stories of Christian leaders who, 13–17, 58, 60–61, 63–65
Integrity, 97
InterVarsity Christian Fellowship, 13–14
Israelites, 56, 57, 88

Jeremiah: 33, 56; 45:5, 71
Jerusalem, 57
Jesus: crucifixion of, 65, 75–76, 88–89; feet washing of, 109; great commandments of, 108; humility of, 72–73; mission of, 107; as One Minute Manager, 102; psychological hardiness and, 77–78; relational leadership of, 119; on sacrifice, 65; as servant leader, 87–88, 97, 101–103, 106, 108, 122–123; suffering of, 75–76, 123; as teacher, 62; vulnerability of, 89–90; wandering of, 111
Jesus Prayer, 22, 63
Jiffy Lube, 16
Joan of Arc, 76
John: 14:10, 73; 15:12–13, 65; 16, 88–89
John the Baptist, 76
Johnson, S., 6, 102, 110
Joseph, M., 44–46, 47–48
Journaling, 13
Joy, 97

Ken Blanchard Companies, 6
Killing the messenger, 105
King, M. L., Jr., 57, 76
Kingdom of God: as Christian vision, 56, 57, 59, 66, 67; modeling faith and, 51–52
Kouzes, J. M., 1, 7, 51, 56, 62, 75, 77, 78, 80, 87, 89, 108, 111, 112, 119, 121
Kuralt, C., 63

Lakeview Middle School, 49–51
Language, of secular and Christian leadership, 55–56

Recognition for contributions: to Encourage the Heart, 34–35, 99, 103–105, 106, 108–109, 111, 112–115; hero stories as, 95–96; high expectations and, 34–35; humility *versus* desire for, 72–75, 104–105, 106; personalized, 35, 112–115; standards and, 108–109

Redemption, sacrifice and, 65, 123

Reflection, 4

Reflection questions: on Challenge the Process, 81; on Enable Others to Act, 98; on Encourage the Heart, 116; on Inspire a Shared Vision, 68; on Model the Way, 52

Relationships and relationship building: celebration of values and, 36, 38; leadership as, 117–124

Repent, meaning of, 67

Results, Encourage the Heart and, 110–115

Resurrection, 88–89

Reverse engineering, 66–67

Rewards, 24; to Encourage the Heart, 33, 111–115

Ridicule, 75–76, 77

Right, catching others doing, 103, 104, 110–115

Risk and risk taking, 22, 24–26, 69, 79–81; helping team members with, 78–81

Rituals: celebration and, 36; Christian, 66; teaching through, 66

Roman emperors, 119

Russell, L., 63

Sacrifice, as soul of leadership, 64–65, 124–125

Safety, trust and, 89

Sage, J., 13–17

Saints, 76

1 Samuel, 93–94

Saviors, 55

School leaders, 49–51

Schuller, R., 102

Scripture: study of, 115; teaching from, 46–47

Seeing: and believing, 57–59; learning through, 65–66

Self-absorption, 104–105

Self-development, 122

Self-disclosure, 89–90

Self-esteem: need for external recognition and, 106; psychological hardiness and, 77–78

Selflessness and selfless leadership: Challenge the Process and, 72–75, 81; humil-

ity and, 72–75, 81, 104–105; of Jesus, 72–73; self-serving leadership *versus,* 103–105, 110–111, 115–116; service and, 122–124; suffering and, 124–125

Seminary leadership, 55

Senses, learning through, 65–66

Separations, 78, 79

September 11, 60–61

Servant leadership, 101–116, 122–124; conceptual origins of, 123–124; Enable Others to Act and, 87–88, 96–98; Encourage the Heart and, 101–116; formal positional leadership *versus,* 122–123; Jesus as model for, 87–88, 97, 101–103, 106, 108, 122–123; point of view of, 106–108; vision and, 106–109

Service: humility and, 72–75, 104–105; leadership relationship and, 122–124; selfless, 72–75, 81, 103–105; servant leadership and, 101–116, 122–124; suffering and, 75–78, 124–125

Set the example. *See* Example setting

Share Our Strength Foundation, 58

Shared vision. *See* Inspire a Shared Vision; Vision

Shore, B., 58

Simple Way, The, 86

Smith, F., 47

Society of St. Andrew, 8–10, 11

Soft management, 116

Solitude, 115

Spirit, 67–68

Spirit of community, 99

Spiritual disciplines, 66, 114–115

Standards: Encourage the Heart and, 108–109; recognition and, 34–35. *See also* Expectations

Standards of Excellence for United Way operations, 63–64

Stanford University, 48–49

Stanley, A., 3

Starbucks, 14

Stewardship, 55

Stoner, J., 107

Stories of exemplary leaders, 1–2, 3–4; who Challenge the Process, 19–22, 73–74; who Enable Others to Act, 26–30, 85–87, 91–93, 94–95, 96–97; who Encourage the Heart, 30–38; who Inspire a Shared Vision, 13–17, 58, 60–61, 63–65; who Model the Way, 8–13, 44–46, 47–48, 49–52

Storytelling: to Encourage the Heart, 31–33; epic, 59, 66; for vision sharing, 66

Strengthening others, 29–30, 83, 90–98
Stress: with change, 25; critical incidents and, 13; responses to, 25
Success: celebration of, 36, 38, 99; expectations for, 34–35; incremental improvements and, 80–81; reverse engineering of, 66–67
Suffering: Challenge the Process and, 71–72, 75–78; inspiration and vision from, 56–57, 124–125; psychological hardiness and, 77–78; willingness for, 71–72, 75–78
Sunshine test, 20
Symbolic communication, for vision sharing, 65–68

Table Group, The, 5
Taco Bell, Inc., 62
Talent radar, 93–94
Teaching: doing *versus*, 46–48; nonverbal, 65–66; a vision, 62, 65–68
Team spirit, 67, 83
Teams and teamwork: for Challenge the Process, 78–81; development and life cycles of, 78; Enable Others to Act and, 83, 85–98; incremental improvement and, 80–81; member selection for, 78–79; risk taking in, 79–81; trust and, 89–90
Ten Commitments of Leadership, 37
Thank yous, 34–35, 105
Theme, vision and, 18
Theresa, Mother, 65
2 Timothy 1:6, 95
Trust: fostering collaboration and, 28, 83, 89–90; in God, 97, 115; leading from a servant's heart and, 96–97; power sharing and, 30, 96–97
Truth tellers, 115
21 Irrefutable Laws of Leadership, The (Maxwell), 5, 49

Unconditional love, 106, 115
United Methodist Church, ESL and Immigrant Ministries of, 26–30
United Methodist Church of the Resurrection (COR), 30–34
U. S. Army, 61
U. S. Congressmen, 74–75
U. S. Justice Department, 49–51
United Way of America, 19–23, 63–64
University of Saskatchewan, Extension Division, Business and Leadership Programs, 13

Value statements, 45–46
Values: alignment of, 11–13, 120–121; celebration of, 36, 38, 99; clarity in personal, 10–11; conflict, 107–108; credibility and, 120–121; example setting and, 11–13, 39, 48–52; expressing credibility and, 120–121; finding one's voice and, 10–11, 39, 120–121; forging shared, 11–13, 121; of a godly leader, 97; as guides, 44–55; Model the Way and, 2, 8–13, 39, 41–52; prioritizing, 107–108; servant leaders' vision and, 107–108
Vision: articulating, 59–61; clear and compelling, 108–109; defined, 17; elements of, 107–108; enlisting others in, 18–19, 53, 59–68; envisioning the future and, 17–18; giving life to, 65–68; implementation of, 109; inspiring a shared, 13–19, 53, 55–68; Kingdom of God as, 56, 57, 66, 67; listening deeply and, 62–64; rainbow quality of, 57–59; reflection questions on, 68; servant leadership and, 106–109; suffering as catalyst for, 56–57; teaching, 62; terms for, 17; *theme* and development of, 18; values and, 107–108
Visual learning, modeling and, 48–51
Voice: expressing one's values and, 120–121; finding one's, 10–11, 39
Vulnerability: in giving power away, 29–30; trust and, 89–90

Wall of fame, 114
Wartman, K., 73–74
Washington Monument, Easter services at, 58
Waterman, B., 111
Weakness, power in, 41–42
Weems, L. H., Jr., 62–63
Wesley, J., 60
Wesley Theological Seminary, 5, 22, 55, 121
Whitfield, G., 60
Willow Creek Community Church, 5–6, 85–87, 91–93, 94–95, 96–97
Work, finding meaning in, 18, 24
Work as a Calling (Novak), 93
Worrying, 77–78

Youth camp, 10
Youth ministry, 85–87, 95–96

Zion, 56, 57

Paper 0-7879-6464-6

CREDIBILITY
How Leaders Gain and Lose It,
Why People Demand It

A personal, inspiring, and genuine guide to helping leaders understand the fundamental importance of credibility in building personal and professional success.

THE LEADERSHIP PRACTICES INVENTORY (LPI)

Over its nearly 20-year history, the LPI has become the most popular off-the-shelf 360-degree leadership assessment instrument in the world, used by nearly one million leaders worldwide. Repeated analysis of the instrument has proven it to be a reliable and valid measure of a leader's effectiveness. But most important to its creators, the results have also shown that leadership is understandable and learnable.

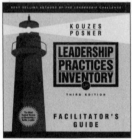

Loose-leaf 0-7879-6728-9

LEADERSHIP PRACTICES
INVENTORY (LPI)
Third Edition

Gives managers and supervisors the skills to master the Five Practices of Exemplary Leadership: Modeling the Way, Inspiring a Shared Vision, Challenging the Process, Enabling Others to Act, and Encouraging the Heart.

LPI ONLINE (www.lpionline.com)

LPI Online is a time-saving, interactive tool for administering the *Leadership Practices Inventory (LPI)*. LPI Online  offers simplified, time-saving administration; immediate, streamlined results; and 24/7 web-based access for LPI administrators and participants.

Learn Anytime, Anywhere

THE FIVE PRACTICES OF EXEMPLARY LEADERSHIP
When Leaders Are at Their Best

This 16-page article is perfect for leaders with limited time and budget. It provides a concise overview of Kouzes and Posner's model and overall thoughts on leadership.

Paper 0-7879-6749-1

THE LEADERSHIP CHALLENGE POSTER, Third Edition

This full-color poster (17" x 22") is the perfect leave-behind prize for participants or reminder tool for organizations that have adopted the Leadership Challenge model. It features *The Five Practices®* and *Ten Commitments of Exemplary Leadership.*

Paper 0-7879-6723-8

THE LEADERSHIP CHALLENGE CARD

This handy pocket-sized card for desks, organizers, and wallets offers quick reference to the model used in *The Leadership Challenge* and the *LPI.*

Paper 0-7879-6571-5

WHAT FOLLOWERS EXPECT FROM LEADERS
How to Meet People's Expectations and Build Credibility
Audio 1-55542-908-4

Make better use of your commute time. These two one-hour audio cassettes provide concrete examples and specific guidance on how to become a more effective leader.

Plan a Leadership Workshop

The Leadership Challenge™ *Workshop*
This intensive two-or three-day program is based on the best-selling book and designed by its authors.

- Offered by the Tom Peters Company in onsite, public, and custom formats with pre- and post-consulting available for ongoing needs.

- Implemented by some of the world's most recognized companies, including Brooks Brothers, Cisco, Clorox, Rolls-Royce, Seagate Technology, Sun Microsystems, Unilever, and Wells Fargo Bank.

Leadership Is Everyone's Business™
A one-day workshop that develops the leadership practices of individual contributors at all levels of the organization.

To learn more about these learning opportunities, contact the Tom Peters Company in the U.S. and abroad at 888-221-8685, e-mail info@tompeters.com, or visit their website at www.tompeters.com/implementation/solutions/challenge.

Get Connected With the Convenience of Online Learning

Playback Media
In partnership with Playback Media, Kouzes and Posner have created five online courses—*Enabling Others to Act, Encouraging the Heart, Modeling the Way, Inspiring a Shared Vision,* and *Challenging the Process.* They are delivered live, on the Web, at very affordable prices.

To learn more, visit www.playbackmedia.com.

Instigo
Working with Instigo, Jim Kouzes produced several highly interactive online seminars. They are now available to you and your organization for your next learning activity.

To learn more, visit www.instigo.com.

Create Excitement with
The Leadership Challenge Video Collection

Video programs offer a compelling format for leadership training in both small groups and large gatherings. These *Leadership Challenge* videos are designed to educate, inspire, and liberate the leader in everyone.

Leadership Challenge: This compelling video shows that leadership is attainable; it is not the private preserve of a few charismatic people but a learnable set of practices.

Leadership in Action: Based on the best-selling book *The Leadership Challenge,* this must-have video describes the five practices common to all successful leaders through a single case study.

Closing the Leadership Gap: This exceptional video reveals how to cultivate and maintain credibility and fill the leadership gap—when leaders say one thing and do another.

Encouraging the Heart: This video illustrates the importance of employee recognition and presents examples of the types of rewards leaders can give to truly motivate top performance.

Credibility: This two-part video series explores the difference between a person in a leadership position, and a person whose direction you are willing to follow.

The Credibility Factor: This program explores the relationship between leaders and their followers, and details the ingredients necessary for quality leadership.

To learn more, visit www.crmlearning.com or call 800-421-0833.

JOSSEY-BASS
An Imprint of
🖑 **WILEY**

Pfeiffer
A Wiley Imprint
www.pfeiffer.com